The Power of Connecting:
From Friends to Great Leaders

Ezra Muri

Copyright © 2025 Ezra Muri

All rights reserved.

ISBN: **978-1-0694802-0-0**

"The greatest power is neither controlled nor imposed --- it is shared. It is born when we choose to connect with the heart… and serve with the soul."

-Ezra Muri-

DEDICATION

To those who have felt the weight of loneliness, who have desired authentic connection but didn't know how to achieve it; to those who have doubted their ability to be heard, understood and valued. This book is for you.
May these pages be a reminder that it is never too late to build bridges, that the desire to connect is a brave step toward transformation. We all have the ability to create bonds that illuminate our lives and those of others.
With love and hope, this book belongs to you.

Index

The Importance of Connecting with Empathy------------------------ 15
The Power of Active Listening--------------------------------------17
Authenticity: The Key to Lasting Relationships------------------------19
Practical Exercise: Building Meaningful Relationships Through Presence and Intention----------------------------------21
    1. Choose a Relationship You Wish to Nurture------------21
    2. Practice Active and Conscious Listening----------------21
    3. Offer a Heartfelt Act of Kindness-------------------------- 22
    Final Reflection: The Invisible Ecosystem of Connection--23
The Essence of Positive Influence------------------------------------ 25
The Importance of Listening and Understanding----------------------27
Building Relationships Based on Trust---------------------------------- 29
Practical Strategies to Positively Influence-------------------------------31
Angela Merkel and her Trust-Based Leadership---------------------- 32
Practical Exercise: Cultivating Your Influence Through Empathy and Purpose--33
    1. Identify a Key Relationship in Your Life------------------ 33
    2. Listen with Attentiveness and True Presence---------- 34
    3. Act from Your Values: Be an Inspiration, Not a Persuasion---35
    Final Reflection: The Invisible Impact of Your Presence 35
The Essence of Connected Leadership-------------------------------- 37
Building Cohesive Teams-- 39
Satya Nadella and the Construction of Cohesionated Equipment-41
Inspiring Through Narrative--- 43
Empathy as a Leadership Tool---45
Practical Strategies for Connected Leadership-------------------------- 48
    1. Evaluate the Level of Connection with Your Team or Community-- 49
    2. Practice Active Listening with the Intention to

Understand---49
3. Share a Story that Inspires Unity---50
Final Reflection: To Lead is to Build Bonds that Transform 50

Understanding the Origin of Conflicts---53
The Importance of Empathy in Conflict Resolution---56
Transform Conflicts into Opportunities---59
Practical Strategies to Resolve Conflicts---62
Practical Exercise: Turning Conflict into a Bridge for Growth---62
   1. Identify a Current Conflict and Observe It Clearly---63
   2. Explore Creative Solutions with Emotional Awareness-63
   3. Choose One Action and Apply It with Empathy---64
   Final Reflection: The Power to Heal Through Conflict---64

The Evolution of Relationships: From Personal Connections to Professional Alliances---67
Building Alliances Based on Shared Values---69
Overcoming Challenges in Professional Relationships---71
Practical Exercise: Transforming Friendships into Purposeful Alliances---74
   1. Identify a Friendship with Collaborative Potential---74
   2. Establish a Shared Purpose---75
   3. Design a Conscious Action Plan---76
   Final Reflection: When Friendship Becomes a Creative Force---76

The Essence of Authentic Communication---77
Listen to Connect---81
Vulnerability as Strength---84
Practical Strategies for Authentic Communication---87
Practical Exercise: Elevating Your Communication Through Authenticity---88
   1. Reflect Honestly on Your Communication Style---88
   2. Practice Active Listening as a Form of Presence---89
   3. Share a Personal Story with Intention---89
   Final Reflection: Communicating to Connect, Not Just to

Be Heard---90
The Importance of Inspiration---91
The Battle of May 5th: Ignacio Zaragoza and His Power To Inspire To Others---94
Building Trust Through Coherence---96
The Power of Recognition---99
Practical Strategies to Get Others to Follow You---101
Practical Exercise: Cultivating Soulful, Inspirational Leadership---101
   1. Define a Vision That Goes Beyond Yourself---101
   2. Identify the Values That Anchor Your Path---102
   3. Acknowledge and Appreciate Those Who Walk Beside You---102
   Final Reflection: Leading with Purpose, Integrity, and Love---103
Understanding Emotional Intelligence: The Key to Leadership and Authentic Relationships---105
Self-awareness: Know Yourself---106
Self-regulation: Manage Your Emotions with Intelligence---107
Motivation: The Engine that Will Drive You to Continue Growing---107
Empathy: Connecting with Others on a Deeper Level---108
Social Skills: Build Relationships with Emotional Intelligence---108
Self-awareness and Self-regulation: The Foundation of Personal Leadership---110
Empathy as a Pillar of Emotional Intelligence---112
Empathy is the invisible bridge that unites people, the silent language that says "I see you, I hear you, I understand you". At the heart of emotional intelligence, empathy is the skill that allows us to connect with others on a deep level, understand their emotions, and respond sensitively. It is not just about sympathizing with the other, but about putting yourself in their place, feeling what they feel and acting with understanding. In a world where communication has become instantaneous, but often superficial, developing empathy is more important than ever.-- 112
Emotional Intelligence as an Essential Skill---113
Lead from Service---115

Building Trust Through Coherence-------------------------------- 117
Inspiring with Purpose-- 119
Your Commitment as a Leader---------------------------------- 121
Reflecting on the Power of Connection------------------------ 123
Leadership as a Commitment to Others------------------------ 125
Your Next Steps as a Connected Leader------------------------127
Final Exercise: Your Manifesto of Connection and Leadership 127
    1. Write Your Purpose as a Conscious Leader---------- 128
    2. Identify Your Guiding Principles-------------------------- 128
    3. Make a Concrete Commitment to Action-------------- 129
Final Reflection: Your Manifesto Is Alive---------------------- 129
A Commitment to Lead with Impact---------------------------------130

Acknowledgments

This book, *The Power of Connecting*, is the result of a journey full of learning, challenges and, above all, unconditional love and support. To each person who has been part of this path, my deepest gratitude.

To my parents, who with their love and example taught me the value of empathy and the importance of human relationships. Their guidance and support have been instrumental in making me who I am today.

To my closest friends, whose nobility and potential inspired me to write these pages. Thank you for being a constant reminder that we all have within us the ability to lead and connect with others. This book is, in part, for you and for all the people who, like you, seek to overcome their limitations to become the best version of themselves.

To every person who, at some point, trusted me during my years as a holistic therapist. Thank you for opening your heart and allowing me to be part of your healing and transformation process. Each of their stories taught me something valuable that I carry with me.

To Canada, a country that challenged me to grow and gave me the opportunity to connect with people from all over the world. This place, with its multiculturalism, was the perfect setting to hone the skills and lessons I share in this book.

To my readers, present and future, who have decided to take this journey with me. Thank you for trusting my message and for allowing me to be part of your transformation. My greatest hope is that these pages ignite a spark of inspiration in you and guide you toward a more connected and meaningful life.

Finally, thanks to life itself, which has given me the opportunity to learn, fail, grow and share. Every experience, both the sweet and the bitter, has been an invaluable teacher.

This book is not just mine, but belongs to all those who have walked with me. To you, with love and eternal gratitude, I dedicate these words.

Introduction:

The Path to Meaningful Connections

Imagine for a moment that you have the power to transform every interaction you have into a memorable experience. May your words, your gestures, and your actions build bridges of trust and friendship with those around you.

No matter who you are or where you are, this power is within your reach. In this book, I want to invite you to discover how genuine connections can change your life and how you can become a leader who inspires others to follow your example.

Human relationships are certainly the core of our existence. Whether in our personal or professional lives, our ability to connect with others largely determines the quality of our experiences. However, building meaningful relationships is not always easy.

In a world moving at breakneck speed, where digital interactions often replace face-to-face encounters, the art of winning friends and leading with empathy has become an invaluable skill.

This book is not a quick formula manual or a set of generic advice. It is a thoughtful and practical guide designed to help you understand and apply the fundamental principles that form the core of human relationships.

Together we will explore topics such as empathy, authenticity, active listening and the ability to inspire. I will tell you stories of extraordinary people who, through their ability to connect and lead, have changed lives and transformed the world.

But more importantly, this book is designed for you. I want you to feel like every word is directed to you, that every idea resonates with you, and that every chapter is one step closer to the leader you are destined to be. It doesn't matter if you consider yourself an extrovert or an introvert, whether you are just starting your leadership journey or already have years of experience: this book has something to offer you.

At the end of each chapter, you will find practical exercises that will help you apply the concepts we have discussed. These exercises are not homework; They are opportunities to reflect, grow, and put into practice what you are learning. I want you to see this book not just as a read, but as a transformative experience.

Prepare to embark on a journey that will not only change how you relate to others, but also how you see yourself. Because when you connect from the heart, lead with purpose, and act with integrity, the impact you can have on the world is limitless. Now, let's take the first step together.

Throughout this book, I have included brief stories of extraordinary people who have demonstrated the power of meaningful connections and authentic leadership. As you read their stories, reflect on how their actions and principles can apply to your life. They are a reminder that we all have the power to make a difference, no matter our circumstances.

Chapter 1:

The Art of Winning Friends

Think about one of the people closest to you. Do you remember how your friendship began? Maybe it was a moment of shared empathy, a meaningful conversation, or an unexpected act of kindness. True friendships don't happen by accident; They are the result of small actions that demonstrate genuine interest, respect and authenticity.

In this first chapter, I want to invite you to reflect on the importance of winning friends and how this act can enrich your life in ways you may not have considered. Winning friends is not an end in itself; It is a path to meaningful relationships that can open doors, offer support, and ultimately make life more fulfilling and satisfying.

The Importance of Connecting with Empathy

Connecting with empathy is much more than a social skill; It is an act of humanity that transforms how we understand and relate to others. In a world where haste and superficiality often reign, empathy invites us to stop and look beyond the words, towards the feelings that inspire them. It reminds us that behind every face there is a story, a struggle, a dream. And when we allow ourselves to listen with our hearts, we not only connect with others, but we also discover parts of ourselves.

Have you ever felt the relief of being understood without having to explain too much?

That is the magic of empathy. It is looking someone in the eyes and saying, without words: *"I see you, I hear you, you matter"*. It is the tool that dismantles barriers and transforms disagreements into points of understanding. Instead of judging, the act of connecting with empathy leads us to ask: *"How can I be here for you?"* And it is in that question where the deepest and most authentic relationships are born.

Imagine a leader who not only listens, but feels his team's concerns as if they were his own. That leader not only directs; inspire. When we lead from empathy, people feel valued and seen, and that not only creates more united teams, but also happier and more engaged. Empathy is that universal language that unites us, regardless of our differences, and that reminds us that we all share the desire to be understood.

In personal life, empathy becomes the glue that holds our most important relationships together. It's when we sit next to a friend on their worst day and, even if we don't have the perfect words, we are present with our soul.

It's that silent hug, that look of support, those small actions that say: *"You are not alone"*. When we open ourselves to feeling what others feel, we create a space where emotions flow freely and love finds its home.

Connecting with empathy transforms us. It allows us to see the beauty in vulnerability, the strength in understanding, and the power of uniting hearts despite differences.

In a world that often pushes us toward disconnection, choosing empathy is an act of resistance, hope, and love. Because at the end of the day, what we remember most are not the facts, but the human connections that made us feel alive.

What could be more valuable than that?

Connecting with others begins with the ability to understand and value their perspectives. Empathy is the bridge that bridges differences and creates common ground where relationships can flourish. When we listen carefully and respond sensitively, we send a clear message:

"I value you and I care about what you think and feel".

Think about the words of **Dale Carnegie**, author of *"How to Win Friends and Influence People,"* who said:

"You can win more friends in two months by being genuinely interested in others than in two years trying to get them interested in you."

Carnegie transformed the way people approach relationships and leadership. His legacy lies in demonstrating that genuine concern for others is the most effective path to building friendships and gaining influence.

"Empathy not only builds relationships; it also builds trust and respect with those around you."
-Ezra Muri-

The Power of Active Listening

Active listening is much more than paying attention; It is one of the deepest forms of human connection we can offer. In a world where everyone wants to be heard, but few truly feel understood, active listening becomes a transformative act. It is telling the other, without words: *"I'm here for you. You matter. I see you."*

How many times have you wished that someone would really listen to you?

That feeling of relief and courage is what you can give to others with this powerful skill.

The magic of active listening lies in its simplicity and depth. It's not about offering quick solutions or interrupting with our own stories, but about being present. For a moment, we forget our worries and focus all our attention on the person in front of us. And in that act, we open a space where emotions can flow freely, where the other person feels valued and understood.

Now I'm going to ask you:

When was the last time someone listened to you with all their heart?

Imagine how wonderful it can be to become that beacon of empathy for someone else.

Active listening is also an act of courage. It invites us to look beyond the words, to perceive the emotions that are hidden behind them. It's an opportunity to connect with another person's humanity, even when we don't share their experiences or points of view. It doesn't mean agreeing, but understanding. And in that understanding, we find the power to heal relationships, resolve conflicts, and build bridges where before there were only walls.

When you actively listen, something magical happens: the other person feels seen. Imagine the impact of truly listening to a friend who is going through a bad time, a child who is trying to express themselves, or a colleague who needs to be appreciated. That simple act can change not only their day, but also their perception of themselves and their relationships. Because when we listen with our hearts, we remind them that they are not alone, that their words have weight, and that their existence matters.

The impact is not only external; Active listening also transforms us. It teaches us to be more patient, to empathize deeply, and to connect with the very essence of what it means to be human. Every time you choose to actively listen, you choose to build instead of destroy, unite instead of separate.

So the next time someone talks to you, turn off the noise in your mind, look them in the eyes and listen. You don't know the power you have to change their world and, perhaps, yours too.

Listening is not the same as hearing. Active listening involves paying full attention to the other person, processing what they say, and responding thoughtfully. This skill, although simple in appearance, is one of the most powerful you can develop.

An inspiring example is that of **Mahatma Gandhi**, Leader of the Indian independence movement. His ability to listen to and understand the communities he led was key to his success because he spent time listening to the farmers and workers of India.

By understanding their struggles and needs, he not only gained their trust, but also strengthened their movement for justice and freedom. Gandhi teaches us that active listening not only transforms relationships; It also has the power to change the course of history. Remember, listening is not just an act; *It's a gift*.

What are you waiting for to share it?

Authenticity: The Key to Lasting Relationships

Being authentic is an act of bravery in a world that often pushes us to fit in, to show only what we think others want to see. But authenticity is much more than being **"oneself"**; It is a commitment to truth, to transparency, and to accepting who you are, even when it is not perfect. It is in that honesty where the deepest and most lasting relationships flourish.

Have you ever felt the relief of being accepted just as you are?

That is the power of authenticity: it liberates and connects.

Authentic relationships are not built on masks or appearances, but on open hearts. When we are genuine, we give others permission to be genuine too. It's like saying: *"Here I am, with my virtues and defects. Do you also dare to show yourself?"* And in that honest exchange, an unbreakable bond is created, one that depends not on perfection, but on shared truth. Authenticity doesn't attract everyone, but it does attract the right people, those who truly deserve to be in your life.

Being authentic also means being vulnerable, and that vulnerability is what makes relationships real. When you share your fears, your dreams, and your challenges, you are saying: *"'I trust you enough to show you who I really am."* And that trust is the foundation of any lasting relationship.

Do you remember the last time someone was completely honest with you?

Probably you felt inspired, maybe even relieved. That is the transformative power of authenticity.

In a world where social media and appearances often dictate how we should be, choosing authenticity is a revolutionary act. Being authentic doesn't mean sharing everything about yourself with everyone, but rather carefully choosing the people with whom you want to build real, deep connections. It's learning to say *"this is me"* proudly, without fear of judgment or comparison. Because when you allow yourself to be yourself, you also attract those who value that truth, and those are the relationships that really matter.

Authenticity not only enriches our relationships with others, but also the relationship we have with ourselves. By being true to who we are, we find inner peace and security that no external approval can give us.

So I ask you:

What would happen if today you chose to be completely authentic?

You may find that the relationships you build, when they are rooted in your truth, are not only stronger, but also more meaningful and lasting. Authenticity isn't just the key to relationships; It is the heart of a full life.

Being authentic means being yourself, without masks or pretensions. When you show yourself as you are, with your strengths and weaknesses, you allow others to do the same. Authenticity creates a safe space where relationships can develop with honesty and depth.

Fred Rogers, known as "Mister Rogers," is a moving example of authenticity in action. His ability to connect with children and adults through his television show came not from tricks or artifice, but from his genuine interest and respect for each person. Rogers reminds us that authenticity is not only attractive; It is transformative.

Practical Exercise: Building Meaningful Relationships Through Presence and Intention

Authentic connections don't happen by chance. They're built—step by step—through intention, presence, and a willingness to open up to others. This exercise is designed to help you deepen a relationship with someone important in your life, but also to reconnect with yourself. Because every bond we transform outwardly begins with a shift within.

---

1. Choose a Relationship You Wish to Nurture

Think of someone with whom you feel there's untapped potential:

- Perhaps a friend you've drifted away from.

- A family member you'd like to reconnect with in a healthier way.

- A colleague you sense a deeper connection with beyond the professional realm.

Take a moment to close your eyes and visualize this person.
What do you feel when you think of them? What would you like to heal, strengthen, or rediscover?

Make this choice not out of duty, but from a genuine desire to show up with an open heart.

---

2. Practice Active and Conscious Listening

Most people listen to reply—not to understand.
In your next interaction with this person, choose to truly listen.
This means:

- Put your phone away.

- Maintain gentle eye contact.

- Notice not just the words, but also the pauses, the gestures, and the energy behind what is said.

Ask open-ended questions that invite depth:

- *What's been most meaningful to you in recent months?*

- *Is there something you'd like to share that you feel few people understand?*

- *How have you really been feeling lately?*

Don't interrupt. Don't try to "fix" anything. Just be there.
Sometimes, being fully heard is the most profound act of love someone can receive.

---

3. Offer a Heartfelt Act of Kindness

This isn't just a random "nice gesture."
It's something that silently says: ***"I'm here with you. I value you. I see you."***

Think of something that aligns with what this person values:

- A handwritten note recognizing their strength.

- A symbolic gift that represents a shared memory.

- An honest, vulnerable message expressing what you admire about them.

It doesn't have to be grand.
What matters most is that it's **genuine** and **aligned with your intention**.

Final Reflection: The Invisible Ecosystem of Connection

Once you've completed these three steps, pause and feel...
What shifted?
Did the energy between you feel different?
Did you notice a softness in their voice, a spark in their eyes, a different kind of silence?

And beyond what happened with the other person, ask yourself:

- What did I discover about myself by choosing to be more present and human?

- What part of me opened up through this vulnerability or attentiveness?

- What fears did I let go of, and what new ways of connecting did I explore?

This exercise is not just a practice—it's a doorway.
A doorway to a new kind of relationship: more conscious, more empathetic, more transformative.

And this chapter is only the beginning.

As we move forward, we'll explore not just how to connect more deeply with others, but how to heal what blocks us from doing so.
Because in the art of connection, the soul reveals itself—and the world transforms.

Are you ready to step into relationships rooted in soul, truth, and purpose?

Chapter 2:

How to Positively Influence Other People

Positively influencing others is a skill that transcends persuasion or convincing. It is the ability to inspire, motivate and guide those around you towards a shared purpose. This chapter is designed to help you understand how you can impact the lives of others in meaningful ways by fostering relationships based on trust, respect, and mutual value.

The Essence of Positive Influence

Positively influencing the lives of others is one of the greatest gifts we can offer the world. True influence is not about manipulating or imposing, but about inspiring, guiding and leaving a mark that uplifts those around us. It is a silent but powerful force, one that transcends words and actions, reaching directly to the hearts of people.

Have you ever felt how a single person, by their example or words, transformed your perspective?

That is positive influence: a change that is born from the soul.

The essence of positive influence lies in example. People don't follow what we say, they follow what we do. When we live by our values, we show the world what integrity, empathy, and purpose mean. That coherence is magnetic, because it invites us to trust, to believe in something greater.

What kind of example are you setting in your daily life?

Perhaps without knowing it, you are already inspiring someone who looks at you with admiration.

Being a positive influence also means listening more than we talk and understanding before judging. It is taking the time to recognize the challenges of others, to encourage them rather than criticize them, and to remind them of their value when they themselves have forgotten it.

What impact would it have on the people around you if you reminded them today how important they are?

Sometimes a gesture as simple as a word of encouragement can change the direction of a life.

Positive influence is not a task reserved for great leaders or public figures; It is something that we all carry inside. Every interaction is an opportunity to leave an impact.

It can be as simple as a genuine smile, or as profound as extending your hand when someone else needs it. Never underestimate the power of your small actions; It is those actions that build bridges and transform lives.

Think about a person who has deeply impacted your life. Maybe it was a teacher who believed in you, a friend who motivated you to keep going during a difficult time, or a leader who inspired you by example. Positive influence is not about imposing our will, but rather creating a space where others can grow and thrive.

An emblematic example of positive influence is **Martin Luther King Jr.**, who led the civil rights movement in the United States. King not only mobilized millions with his iconic speech ***"I Have a Dream"***, but also lived the principles he preached, inspiring people of all races and ages to join his fight for equality. His influence lay in his ability to articulate a clear vision of justice and freedom, combined with deep personal integrity.

Ultimately, positively influencing not only benefits others, it also transforms us. It makes us more aware, more present and more connected to our humanity. It reminds us that, in a world full of challenges, each of us has the power to be a beacon of light for someone else.

So, I ask you:

What influence are you leaving on the people around you?

The answer will not only define your impact on others, but also the legacy you will build with each small act of kindness and leadership.

The Importance of Listening and Understanding

Listening and understanding are not simple skills, they are acts of love, empathy, and connection. In a world full of noise, where everyone seems to be talking, but few are actually listening, stopping to listen deeply is an extraordinary gift. Listening is not just hearing words; It is opening your heart to understand the emotions, fears, and dreams behind them. It is telling the other: *"I see you, I hear you, and what you have to say matters."*

How many times have you longed for that feeling of being completely understood?

Now imagine being able to offer that same gift to someone else.

When we listen with true intention, we create a space where people feel valued and safe. It is not about having all the answers, but about being present, offering our time and attention without interruptions.

Think about that moment when someone really listened to you, without judging, without rushing you. How did you feel? That connection can change not just a conversation, but an entire relationship. Because when we listen to understand, we are building bridges instead of putting up walls.

Listening is also an act of humility. It is recognizing that we do not have all the answers and that we can always learn something from others. It is a door to empathy, a path to put ourselves in the other's shoes and understand their world from their perspective.

Analyze it for a moment:

What could you discover if you chose to listen more and talk less today?

You will likely find that the unsaid words are just as important as those expressed, and that silence can be the bridge to a deeper connection.

The understanding that comes from listening is transformative. Not only does it strengthen our relationships, but it also has the power to heal wounds, resolve conflicts, and bring us closer to others in ways we never imagined.

Listening and understanding not only benefits the other; We enrich ourselves, expanding our capacity to feel, to connect, and to live with greater purpose. Because every time we listen, we are saying: *"Your story matters, and I am here for you, to listen to it."*

Oprah Winfrey, known for its ability to connect with people, is a clear inspiring example in this regard. Throughout her career as an interviewer, Oprah demonstrated a unique ability to listen deeply, creating a space where her guests felt understood and valued. This ability not only strengthened her influence, but also made her a trusted figure for millions of people around the world.

Influence begins with listening. When we take the time to understand the perspectives, needs and aspirations of others, we build a bridge of empathy and connection. Active listening not only strengthens relationships; It also allows us to tailor our message in a way that resonates with those around us.

Ultimately, listening and understanding remind us that we are not alone in this world. It teaches us that words can be powerful, but true connection comes from mutual understanding. So today, choose to be that person who listens with an open heart, who seeks to understand before responding.

You may not always have the perfect words, but your presence will be enough to brighten someone's day. And maybe, just maybe, in that act of listening, you'll find a little more of yourself, too.

Building Relationships Based on Trust

Trust is the lifeblood of every meaningful relationship. It is that invisible thread that unites people, that feeling that allows us to let our guard down and show ourselves as we are. Building relationships based on trust doesn't happen overnight; It is a process that requires intention, consistency and, above all, authenticity.

Have you ever felt the comfort of knowing that you can count on someone no matter the circumstances?

That is the strength of trust: a refuge in the midst of chaos.

When you build trust, you are creating a space where people feel safe to be vulnerable, to express themselves without fear of judgment. This type of connection is not about being perfect, but about being honest. It means admitting mistakes when we make them, keeping our promises, and being consistent in what we say and do.

Let's think about it for a moment:

Are you building that security in your relationships? Are you that person that others can fully trust?

Trust also involves listening with an open heart and acting with integrity. It is a continuous commitment to demonstrate with actions what our words promise. When people know they can trust you, something magical happens: barriers disappear, bonds strengthen, and relationships flourish. Because trust doesn't just connect people; it transforms them, creating bonds that can resist any adversity.

Imagine what you could achieve if every relationship in your life was built on a solid foundation of trust. Your friendships would be deeper, your professional connections more productive, and your family relationships more meaningful.

But this doesn't happen by accident; It happens when we choose to be intentional, when we dedicate ourselves to being consistent and transparent in every interaction. Being a person others trust is one of the greatest gifts you can offer them.

Trust is the foundation of all lasting influence. Without it, even the brightest ideas can be discarded. Building trust takes time, consistency, and a genuine interest in the well-being of others.

Mahatma Gandhi. He exemplified this principle by leading the Indian independence movement. His commitment to nonviolence and his willingness to live by the values he promoted earned him the trust of millions.

Gandhi did not ask others to make sacrifices that he himself was not willing to make, which reinforced his credibility and amplified his influence.

In the end, building relationships based on trust not only benefits others; It also transforms us. It frees us from the burden of appearances, helps us find security in ourselves, and allows us to live with greater purpose and peace.

So today, choose to be that trustworthy person, that rock for those around you. Remember, trust is not a luxury; It is the basis of every relationship worth maintaining.

What are you doing today to build it?

Practical Strategies to Positively Influence

Connect with the Values of Others: Discover what is important to the people around you and use that knowledge to construct a message that resonates with them.

   o Example: If you are leading a project, identify how each team member can contribute meaningfully, aligning their talents with the group's objectives.

Be a Role Model: Actions speak louder than words. Live according to the principles you preach.

   o Example: If you value honesty, make sure you are transparent and consistent in your interactions.

Offers Genuine Recognition: Appreciating and recognizing the achievements of others strengthens relationships and motivates people to move forward.

   o Example: A sincere thank you for a coworker's effort can make a big difference in their day.

Angela Merkel and her Trust-Based Leadership

Angela Merkel, known as the "Chancellor of the Free World", stood out for her unique leadership style, deeply rooted in trust.

During her 16 years at the helm of Germany, Merkel not only led a nation, but also became a global symbol of stability, integrity, and empathy. In a political landscape full of noise and empty promises, she chose a quiet but powerful approach: building trust through consistency and transparency.

From the beginning of her mandate, Merkel understood that trust is not demanded, it is earned. She did not seek to impress with grandiose speeches, but with consistent actions and decisions based on clear values.

In times of crisis, such as the global economic recession of 2008 or the migration crisis of 2015, her leadership was defined by her ability to act with calm, clarity, and determination. Instead of looking for quick or popular solutions, she opted for difficult but ethically correct decisions, showing her people that they could trust her judgment even in the darkest moments.

A moment that encapsulates her trust-based leadership was her handling of the immigration crisis. As other leaders closed borders, Merkel spoke the words that would define her legacy: **"We will make it"** (Wir schaffen das). With this statement, she not only reaffirmed her commitment to helping refugees, but also sent a message to the Germans: **"I trust you to face this challenge together."**

Although she faced criticism, her consistency and conviction allowed Germany to lead with humanity at a time when others chose fear.

Merkel was also an example of how humility strengthens confidence. She never sought the center of attention or used her position to impose her will. Instead, she listened, negotiated, and worked to build consensus. This approach not only won the trust of her country, but also that of international leaders, who valued her calm and rational perspective.

And it was precisely this trust that allowed Merkel to be a key mediator in global conflicts and a champion of international cooperation.

Angela Merkel's leadership teaches us that trust is not built with empty words, but with consistent actions and unwavering values. Their example inspires us to lead from a place of integrity, to make difficult decisions when necessary, and to demonstrate with every action that we are worthy of the trust of those around us.

How can you apply this principle in your life?

Perhaps it is time to lead with the same calm, humility, and conviction that defined Merkel and left an indelible mark on the world.

Practical Exercise: Cultivating Your Influence Through Empathy and Purpose

Influence is not manipulation.

True influence is born from the alignment between what you think, feel, and do. It arises from your example, your presence, and your ability to inspire others not through persuasion, but through who you are.
This exercise invites you to practice influence from a place of authenticity, integrity, and genuine human connection.

1. Identify a Key Relationship in Your Life

Think of someone with whom you would like to make a meaningful, positive impact:

- Perhaps a colleague who could use some motivation.
- A friend going through a tough time.
- A loved one who may benefit from a new perspective.

Don't choose from a place of ego, but from a sincere desire to support, to uplift, to walk beside—not ahead of—them.

Pause for a moment. Breathe.
Visualize this person.
What would you love to plant in their life? What qualities do you

admire in them? What values of your own do you want to reflect in the way you relate to them?

---

2. Listen with Attentiveness and True Presence

Every deep influence begins with deep listening.
To listen with an open heart is to say without words: **"You matter. Your inner world matters."**

Dedicate time to be with that person—not just physically, but fully present.
Ask questions that open doors, not judgments:

- *How have you been feeling lately when it comes to…?*

- *What's been inspiring or frustrating you recently?*

- *Where in your life do you feel stuck, even though you want to move forward?*

Observe their body language, their pauses, their tone.
Sometimes, simply being fully present is the beginning of a profound shift in someone's life.

---

3. Act from Your Values: Be an Inspiration, Not a Persuasion

The most powerful influence comes through example.
Find a way to support, encourage, or accompany this person that reflects your deepest values:

- Do you value compassion? Then offer genuine understanding.

- Do you believe in human potential? Remind them of what they're capable of.

- Do you stand for authenticity? Share your own struggles too.

Sometimes, a heartfelt conversation, a thoughtful suggestion, a generous act—or even a respectful silence—can be a catalyst for powerful transformation.

Final Reflection: The Invisible Impact of Your Presence

Once you've completed this exercise, take a moment to reflect:

- What changed in your connection with this person?

- What shifted within you, simply by choosing to observe, to listen, and to act with intention?

- What did you learn about your own capacity to influence without needing to control?

Remember:
Authentic influence is not about changing others—it's about inspiring them to become the best version of themselves.

And to do that, you don't need to force anything.
You only need to be fully present, be yourself, and lead with heart.

This exercise is a chance to bring the principles of this chapter into your real life.

Through small conscious actions, you can become a force of positive transformation for those around you.

Because in the end, **influence is an act of love in service of someone else's growth.**

Are you ready to be the spark that helps someone else rise into who they were meant to be?

Chapter 3:

Leadership Through Connection

Leading is not just directing; it is to build bridges, inspire trust, and guide people toward a shared purpose. Effective leadership is based on human connection, on the ability to see and value each individual as an essential piece of a whole. In this chapter, we will explore how leadership through connection can transform relationships and mobilize teams toward collective success.

The Essence of Connected Leadership

Connected leadership is much more than leading; it is to unite. It is that unique ability of a leader to inspire, listen and relate deeply to the people around him/her. In a world where technology and the rush increasingly disconnect us, connected leadership reminds us that human relationships are at the heart of all meaningful change.

Have you ever felt the transformative energy of a leader who truly cares about you?

That is the essence of leadership that not only leads, but transforms.

Connected leaders do not place themselves above others; they stand next to them. Recognize that each member of your team, each person you interact with, has a story, a struggle, and a purpose. This leader not only leads from reason, but also **from the heart**, creating an environment where people feel valued, seen and heard.

Let's meditate it for a moment:

What impact would it have on your life if every interaction you had was guided by authentic connection?

The essence of connected leadership lies in empathy. It is the ability to put yourself in the shoes of others and understand their perspectives before making decisions. This approach not only strengthens relationships, but also builds trust and commitment. When people feel that their leader understands their challenges and shares their vision, they are more willing to walk together toward a common goal.

How could you be more empathetic in your leadership relationships?

Maybe the first step is to listen more and talk less.

Connection also implies vulnerability. A connected leader is not afraid to admit mistakes or show his or her own challenges. By doing so, you create a space where others feel safe to be authentic. This honesty fosters a culture of trust, where ideas flow freely and people are willing to give their best. Because when leaders show humanity, they remind their team that we are all on this journey together, learning and growing.

A connected leader understands that power lies not in authority, but in the influence that comes from genuine relationships. This involves not only speaking, but also listening, not only leading, but also serving.

Ernest Shackleton, the Antarctic explorer, is a perfect example of good connected leadership. During his famous expedition aboard the Endurance, his ship became trapped in ice, leaving his crew stranded in extreme conditions.

Shackleton not only led his team to survival, but he did so by establishing deep connections with each member. He organized activities to keep morale high, distributed tasks equitably, and, above all, genuinely cared about everyone's well-being. His leadership not only saved lives, but left a legacy that continues to inspire.

Connected leadership is not just a strategy; **It is a commitment to people**. It is recognizing that success is not measured only by results, but by the relationships we build along the way. It is leading with the purpose of uplifting those around us, of leaving a positive mark on their lives.

What are you doing today to lead in a way that connects, inspires and transforms?

Maybe it's time to take the first step toward leadership that not only leads, but truly connects. Because in the end, a leader who manages through connection not only achieves goals; changes lives.

Building Cohesive Teams

A cohesive team does not happen by chance; It is the result of intentional leadership, strong relationships, and shared purpose. It is like an orchestra where each member plays their instrument with passion, but always in harmony with the others. When teams are cohesive, they become something greater than the sum of their parts. And that kind of unity not only drives success, it transforms the experience of working together.

Have you ever felt the energy of being part of a team like this?

It is powerful, motivating and unforgettable.

The basis of a cohesive team is trust. Without it, ideas do not flow, relationships weaken and conflicts intensify. Leaders who build cohesive teams prioritize creating a safe environment, where each member feels they can express themselves freely without fear of judgment.

Ask yourself:

How are you building trust in the teams you belong to?

Maybe the first step is to listen more, be more accessible, and show that you value every contribution.

In addition to trust, cohesive teams share a clear and meaningful purpose. It is not just about meeting goals, but about understanding *because* Those goals matter. Effective leaders align each member's individual strengths with that common purpose, ensuring that everyone feels like their work has impact. This approach not only motivates, but also creates a sense of belonging. Just think about it:

What could you do today to reinforce purpose in your team?

Maybe a simple conversation about what really matters is the starting point to something much bigger.

Communication is also key to cohesion. In effective teams, communication is open, honest, and constant. Members not only share ideas, but also actively listen and work together to solve problems. Disagreements are not avoided; They are approached with respect, knowing that well-managed conflicts strengthen the team rather than weaken it.

How can you improve communication in your team?

Perhaps It's time to implement regular meetings or create spaces where everyone feels comfortable sharing.

Finally, cohesive teams celebrate successes and learn from failures together. Recognizing achievements, no matter how small, strengthens ties and motivates them to continue moving forward. And when things don't go as expected, a strong team doesn't look for blame; look for solutions. This type of collaborative mindset not only drives performance, but also creates an environment where every member feels like they belong.

Satya Nadella and the Construction of Cohesionated Equipment

When Satya Nadella took over leadership of Microsoft in 2014, the company was facing major challenges. Nimbler competitors and a fragmented internal culture threatened its relevance in a fast-moving technology market. But Nadella, with an approach centered on empathy and collaboration, transformed not only the direction of the company, but also its culture, making it a shining example of how building cohesive teams can revitalize an entire organization.

From the beginning, Nadella understood that real change begins with people. She recognized that Microsoft needed to move beyond a rigid, competitive culture to one based on collaboration and collective growth. Under her leadership, she fostered a mindset of *growth* ("growth mindset") that allowed employees not only to learn from their mistakes, but also to feel valued for their ideas and contributions.

Instead of focusing success on individual achievements, Nadella promoted the idea that the best results come when teams work as one. Her mantra:

> *"Success is not about us, it is about empowering others."*

One of the most representative moments of her leadership was the transformation of Microsoft's flagship product, Office 365, into a cloud-based collaborative platform. This change not only required technological innovations, but also a deeply integrated approach across teams.

Nadella encouraged different departments to work together, breaking down silos that previously made communication and cohesion difficult. This new level of collaboration not only improved the product, but also strengthened the company's internal culture.

Nadella's empathy was key in this process. Instead of imposing changes in an authoritarian manner, she dedicated herself to listening to the concerns and needs of her team. She implemented open and honest communication, where all employees, from the highest levels to the most basic, felt that their voices were heard and valued. This approach not only built trust, but also inspired a sense of belonging among workers.

Another of Nadella's notable achievements was her ability to turn Microsoft's purpose into an engine of cohesion. She clearly defined the company's mission: *"Empower every person and organization on the planet to achieve more."* This purpose, shared by all teams, united employees behind a common vision that transcended products and services. It wasn't just a slogan; It was a call to action that connected each person's daily work with global impact.

Under Nadella's leadership, Microsoft not only regained its relevance in the market, but became one of the most valuable companies in the world. More importantly, Nadella demonstrated that building cohesive teams is not just a business strategy, but a way to lead with empathy, purpose, and humanity.

Her legacy inspires us to ask:

What could we achieve if we worked together with a shared vision and a genuine commitment to our relationships?

The answer, as Nadella taught us, is that there is no limit about what a cohesive team can achieve.

Building a cohesive team takes effort, but the result is worth every second. It's more than working together; it is building a community where people support each other, grow together, and achieve the extraordinary and even the previously considered impossible.

So I dare to ask you:

What are you doing today to build a stronger team?

Because maybe the first step is as simple as expressing your appreciation, listening with intention, or reaffirming the purpose that unites you. Because when teams are cohesive, they not only achieve more; They also discover the best in themselves.

Inspiring Through Narrative

Stories have a power that goes beyond words; They are universal tools that connect, inspire and transform. When a meaningful narrative is told, people not only listen, *feel*. They inspire action, awaken emotions and leave a lasting mark on those who listen to them.

Has a story ever changed the way you think or motivated you to act?

That's what narrative does: it moves hearts and minds in a way that data and facts alone cannot.

Inspiring through storytelling means sharing more than information; it is to convey purpose and meaning. A leader who masters this skill not only gives instructions, but creates a shared vision. People not only understand what they should do, but also *Why* It's important. Stories make goals tangible and challenges become adventures worth facing together.

What story can you tell today that will inspire others to join your cause?

The best narratives are not perfect; They are human. They talk about struggles, failures, and redemption. Leaders who dare to share their own challenges and learnings don't just tell stories; They build connections. These narratives show people that they are not alone in their struggles and that success is not a straight line, but a path full of twists and lessons.

Think about it for a moment and ask yourself the following question:

What part of my story might inspire someone else?

I'm sure that your experience could be the beacon of light that someone else needs to hear to find their own path.

A great example of leadership through narrative is **Barack Obama**. During his presidency, he used personal stories to connect with people from all walks of life. From remembering the hardships of his childhood to sharing anecdotes about everyday people who symbolized the values he stood for, Obama didn't just explain policies; he made them resonate in the hearts of his audience.

Their narratives transformed political debates into human movements, showing that every story, no matter how small, can have an enormous impact.

Telling stories is also a form of empowerment. When you share an inspiring narrative, you are inviting others to become protagonists of their own stories. You are saying: *"If they did it, you can do it too."*

This type of inspiration not only mobilizes, but also transforms. Because stories don't just tell what is possible; They expand our idea of what we can achieve.

Ultimately, inspiring through storytelling is not just a skill; It is a gift you can offer to others. It's a way to show them what could be, to help them see the purpose behind actions, and to connect them to something bigger than themselves.

So:

What story are you going to tell today?

Remember, it's not about telling a perfect story, but about telling a story that leaves a mark. Because at the heart of every great leader is a great storyteller.

Empathy as a Leadership Tool

Empathy is not only a desirable quality in a leader; It is an essential tool for guiding with purpose and building authentic connections. Leading with empathy means looking beyond results and goals to understand the people behind them. It is about putting yourself in the shoes of others, understanding their emotions, their struggles, and their aspirations, and showing that their voices matter.

How many times have you felt like someone really understood you?

That power of deep connection is what defines an empathetic leader.

An empathetic leader transforms the dynamics of their team because they create a safe space where people feel valued and understood. Empathy fosters trust, reduces conflict, and opens the door to genuine collaboration. When team members know that their leader not only listens to them, but also understands them, they work with greater commitment and enthusiasm.

Think about it:

How could you show more empathy in your leadership relationships?

Maybe it all starts with listening, not to respond, but to understand.

Empathy is also key to making fairer and more effective decisions. A leader who understands his team's perspectives and needs can identify solutions that benefit everyone. Instead of imposing its vision, it seeks to create consensus, ensuring that decisions reflect the collective well-being. This approach not only strengthens organizational culture, but also creates a long-term positive impact.

What decisions could you make today if you first considered the emotions and perspectives of others?

Jacinda Ardern, former Prime Minister of New Zealand, is a shining example of how empathy can be a powerful tool for leading in times of crisis. One of the highlights of her leadership occurred in March 2019, following the devastating terrorist attack on two mosques in Christchurch, where 51 people lost their lives.

In a world accustomed to cold and calculated political responses, Ardern stood out for her compassion and humanity, leading with her heart at a time of deep national sadness.

From the beginning, Ardern understood that this was not just an act of terrorism, but an attack on the diversity and unity that defined New Zealand. Instead of focusing solely on political or security strategies, she focused on the human impact. She personally visited the families of the victims, dressed in a hijab as a sign of respect and solidarity with the Muslim community.

In her words and actions, she conveyed a clear message:

> *"We are You."*

These three words not only comforted those affected, but also united a nation under one purpose: to reject hate and embrace empathy.

Ardern also used her platform to amplify the voices of affected communities, ensuring their needs and concerns were heard. In the days following the attack, she led with extraordinary calm, adopting immediate policies to restrict semi-automatic weapons in the country, showing that empathy is not incompatible with decisive action.

This approach not only demonstrated her commitment to the security of her nation, but also sent a global message: leadership is not about reacting to fear, but about responding with compassion and conviction.

One of the most moving moments was her speech at the victims' funeral. In front of a crowd, she said:

> **"The only way to overcome hate is through unity."**

It wasn't just words; It was a call to action for an entire nation. Her authenticity resonated deeply, showing that leadership is not about imposing solutions, but about creating a space where people feel understood and supported.

Ardern's empathetic leadership transformed a national tragedy into a moment of togetherness and reflection. Her ability to lead from the heart, while making strong decisions, inspired not only New Zealand, but the entire world.

Ardern taught us that empathy is not a sign of weakness, but a strength that has the power to heal, connect and mobilize.

Her legacy invites us to reflect:

How can we lead with empathy in our own lives?

Because, as she demonstrated, an empathetic leader doesn't just guide; **transforms the heart of a nation.**

Leading with empathy does not mean avoiding difficult decisions, but facing them with humanity. It is recognizing that people are not productivity machines, but human beings with unique emotions and needs. This type of leadership not only creates better results, but also creates an environment where people feel inspired and valued.

What could you achieve if you led from a place of empathy?

Perhaps you would discover that the true power of the leaders are not in their authority, but in their ability to connect.

Ultimately, empathy when is used as a leadership tool not only transforms teams, but also the leader themselves. It teaches us to be more aware, more patient and more human. It's a reminder that leadership is not just about guiding people toward goals, but also about walking alongside them in the process.

So today, choose to lead with empathy. Listen, understand and connect. Because in a world that requires leaders who make a difference, empathy is not just a tool; It is the very heart of authentic leadership.

Practical Strategies for Connected Leadership

Promote Open Dialogue: Create a space where people feel comfortable sharing ideas and concerns.

   o Example: Organize regular meetings where each team member has the opportunity to speak and be heard.

Recognize Contributions: Valuing individual and collective achievements boosts morale and fosters unity.

o Example: Implement a system to celebrate milestones and achievements, big or small.

Be Accessible and Transparent: Connected leaders are available to their team and communicate their decisions clearly.

o Example: Share frequent updates on projects and goals, and actively listen to team feedback.

Practical Exercise: Leading Through Authentic Connection

True leadership doesn't stem from authority—it flows from connection.
It's not about having all the answers, but about creating spaces where people feel seen, heard, and inspired to bring their best selves forward.

This exercise invites you to strengthen your leadership presence by embracing your humanity, your vulnerability, and your ability to connect on a deeper level.

1. Evaluate the Level of Connection with Your Team or Community

Take a moment to observe your current leadership environment:

- How close are your relationships with the people you lead?

- Do you know what motivates them, what challenges they face, and what hidden talents they carry?

- Do they feel safe enough to be honest with you, to speak their truth?

Make a short list of the people you lead directly.
Next to each name, write one word that describes how you currently perceive that connection: distant, strong, superficial, growing, strained, inspiring…

This step will help you see where bridges are solid—and where new ones need to be built.

---

2. Practice Active Listening with the Intention to Understand

Leadership begins the moment you stop talking and start listening.
Not listening to correct, or to craft a clever reply—but to *understand* another person's inner world.

Schedule time this week for a one-on-one conversation with at least one team member.
It doesn't have to be formal—a walk, a shared break, a quiet moment over coffee.
Ask open-ended questions like:

- *What has been most challenging for you lately in the team?*

- *What makes you feel proud of your work?*

- *What do you think we could improve together?*

Listen with your full presence.
Sometimes, being truly heard is all it takes to reignite someone's trust, motivation, and sense of belonging.

---

3. Share a Story that Inspires Unity

Stories connect more deeply than speeches.
Think of a recent challenge your team overcame—or a meaningful success you experienced together.

Prepare a short story to share in your next team meeting or group setting, highlighting:

- The role each person or department played in that process.

- What lessons were learned collectively.

- How this moment reflects the values your team aspires to embody.

Don't aim only to inspire—aim to reflect their worth.
Help them see how their efforts matter, how they are part of something larger than themselves.

Final Reflection: To Lead is to Build Bonds that Transform

After completing this exercise, pause and ask yourself:

- How did it feel to create space for deeper connection?

- What shifted in the energy of your team or community?

- What did I remember about my *own* purpose as a leader?

Remember:
Leadership isn't just about directing tasks—it's about touching souls.
It's about having the courage to show up as fully human, so that others feel safe to do the same.

When you lead with connection, you don't just impact outcomes—

You impact lives.

Chapter 4:

Resolving Conflicts and Strengthening Bonds

Conflicts are inevitable in any relationship, whether personal or professional. However, an effective leader does not avoid conflicts, but rather approaches them as opportunities to strengthen bonds and foster mutual understanding. In this chapter, we will explore key strategies for managing disagreements constructively, drawing on inspiring stories and practical tools that can transform conflict into growth.

Understanding the Origin of Conflicts

Conflicts are an inevitable part of human interaction, but far from being an obstacle, they can become opportunities for growth and transformation. To resolve them effectively, it is crucial to understand their origin, since many times what appears as a superficial disagreement hides deeper needs, fears, or interests.

Have you ever stopped to ask yourself what is really motivating a conflict you are facing?

Understanding those roots is the first step to building a lasting solution.

At their core, conflicts often arise from differences in perspectives, values or interests. What may seem like a trivial matter to one person may be deeply significant to another. However, these differences are not inherently negative. In fact, when approached with empathy and curiosity, conflicts can reveal new ideas, insights, and ways to strengthen relationships. The key is to look beyond the words and visible actions to identify what is really at stake.

Understanding the origin of a conflict also requires intentional listening. Many times, people do not directly express what they need or feel, whether due to fear, insecurity, or ignorance. By actively listening, we not only capture the words, but also the emotions and nuances that accompany them. This act of mindfulness allows us to connect with the true motivations behind the conflict and approach the situation with greater clarity and compassion.

Another fundamental aspect is recognizing our own role in conflicts.

Are we contributing to the tension with our expectations or assumptions?

Examining our own emotions and motivations helps us approach disagreements more objectively and prevent our emotional reactions from escalating the situation. Reflecting on our actions is not a sign of weakness, but rather a powerful tool to disarm conflicts and transform them into opportunities.

Theodore Roosevelt, 26th President of the United States, is remembered for his dynamic leadership, tireless energy, and ability to bravely face challenges. However, one of the most notable aspects of his legacy was his ability to understand the origins of conflicts and address them with a unique combination of empathy, pragmatism and decisive action.

Roosevelt not only faced conflicts; He sought to understand his roots and used that understanding to build solutions that transformed divisions into opportunities.

An emblematic example of his approach occurred during the coal miners' strike of 1902. At the time, the United States was facing an energy crisis, as coal workers demanded better wages and working conditions, while owners refused to negotiate.

The conflict threatened to paralyze the economy in the dead of winter, leaving millions without heat. Instead of immediately taking sides or imposing an authoritarian solution, Roosevelt decided to intervene in an innovate way: by understanding the concerns of both sides.

Roosevelt invited representatives of labor and ownership to the White House, marking the first time a president had mediated a labor dispute of this magnitude. Instead of imposing his authority, he listened carefully to both sides, seeking to understand not only the immediate demands, but the underlying tensions fueling the conflict.

This approach showed that Roosevelt did not see those involved as adversaries, but rather as necessary parties to reaching a sustainable solution.

His empathy and ability to identify the roots of the problem were key. Roosevelt understood that miners not only wanted higher wages, but also dignity and humane conditions. He also acknowledged that owners feared losing control over their businesses at a time of great economic uncertainty.

Recognizing these concerns, Roosevelt proposed neutral arbitration that allowed both sides to reach an agreement without feeling defeated. This innovative approach resolved the strike and set a precedent for future labor negotiations in the United States.

Roosevelt's approach to understanding the origins of conflict also extended to the international arena. During the Russo-Japanese War in 1905, he played a crucial role as a mediator in peace negotiations. Through his deep understanding of the interests and motivations of both nations, he facilitated the Treaty of Portsmouth, ending the conflict.

His leadership in this process earned him the Nobel Peace Prize, in recognition of his ability to address complex conflicts with a deep understanding of their causes.

Theodore Roosevelt teaches us that understanding the origin of conflicts is essential to resolve them effectively. It is not just about reacting to symptoms, but about identifying the roots of tensions and addressing them with empathy, creativity, and determination. His legacy inspires us to look beyond the surface, listen with intention, and lead with the purpose of building lasting solutions.

What conflicts are you facing today?

Maybe, like Roosevelt, the first step is to stop, listen, and really understand what's underneath. Because when we understand the origin of a conflict, we can transform it into an opportunity to unite and move forward.

> *"Do what you can, with what you have, where you are."*
> -Theodore Roosevelt-

When we understand the source of a conflict, we can approach it from a place of empathy and collaboration rather than confrontation. This does not mean avoiding tensions, but facing them with the intention of finding solutions that benefit both parties. Resolving a conflict at its root not only eliminates the immediate problem, but also strengthens relationships and creates a foundation for more constructive future interactions.

Ultimately, understanding the origin of conflict is an act of leadership and humanity. It is an opportunity to show that, although differences are inevitable, the way we address them defines who we are and the impact we leave on others.

What would happen if instead of avoiding conflicts, we faced them with curiosity and empathy?

Perhaps we would discover that, in them, lies the key to building more authentic and meaningful relationships.

The Importance of Empathy in Conflict Resolution

Empathy is the true art of listening with an open heart and seeing the world through the eyes of another. In every conflict there is an opportunity to learn, grow, and grow closer, but this only happens if we choose to lead with empathy.

When we allow empathy to guide our actions, we transform conflicts into bridges to understanding. Think about a time when someone really stopped to understand you, not just listen to you. How did it make you feel? That is the magic of empathy: it heals, connects and transforms.

Resolving a conflict is not winning an argument; It is uniting hearts. When you stop to listen beyond the words, you discover the emotions and needs hidden behind them. Perhaps what seems like anger is actually a plea for recognition. Maybe what seems like stubbornness is just the fear of being ignored. By showing empathy, you give others something invaluable: the feeling of being seen, heard, and validated.

What impact would it have on your relationships if you started asking more and assuming less?

Empathy is not about agreeing with everything; It's about building bridges where there used to be walls. It is the courage to say: *"I don't agree with you, but I understand why you feel that way, and that matters."*

This simple, but powerful act has the ability to defuse tensions and open a space for dialogue. Because, deep down, we all share the same desire: to be understood. When you lead with empathy, you don't just resolve a conflict; you strengthen a relationship.

The power of empathy lies in its ability to transform not only others, but also yourself. When you choose to understand before you react, you discover a calmness and clarity that allows you to handle even the most difficult situations. You stop seeing conflict as a battle and start seeing it as an opportunity to grow and strengthen your connections.

Take a moment to ask yourself the following:

How can I respond with more compassion in my next interaction?

Perhaps that is the first step to changing not only the dynamics of the conflict, but also that of the relationship.

Nelson Mandela, South Africa's first black president, during negotiations to end apartheid in South Africa, showed extraordinary empathy towards his political opponents. Mandela understood that many Afrikaner leaders feared losing their identity and position in a democratic South Africa. Instead of stoking resentments, Mandela listened to their concerns and proposed solutions that reflected mutual commitment.

This approach included maintaining certain cultural symbols and establishing a coalition government that ensured representation for all. Mandela not only defused the fears of his adversaries, but also built a bridge to national reconciliation. His ability to lead with empathy transformed a divided country into an example of unity and forgiveness.

> **"If you talk to a man in a language he understands, it will reach his head. If you speak in his language, it will reach his heart."**
>
> -Nelson Mandela-

Leading with empathy in conflict resolution is not just a strategy; It is an act of humanity. It is recognizing that behind every disagreement there is a human being with emotions, struggles, and aspirations. It is telling the other: *"Your feelings matter, your perspective matters, you matter."* When you choose to resolve conflicts with empathy, you don't just find solutions; you create a legacy of understanding and unity.

So today, decide to lead with empathy. Be the bridge instead of the wall, the calm instead of the storm, and the connection instead of distance. Because at the end of the day, conflicts do not separate us; it is our lack of empathy that does it. But when we lead with our hearts, we discover that even the most difficult disagreements can become opportunities to grow together and build something stronger.

What could be more powerful than that?

Transform Conflicts into Opportunities

Conflicts, no matter how uncomfortable or challenging they may seem, are doors disguised as problems. Behind every disagreement is an opportunity waiting to be discovered: a chance to learn, to grow, and most importantly, to connect on a deeper level. Transforming conflicts into opportunities is not denying their existence or minimizing their impact; It is choosing to face them with courage and curiosity.

Stop for a moment and introspect yourself based on the following question:

How many times have you found a better solution or a stronger relationship after a well-handled conflict?

That is the true essence of growth.

Instead of seeing conflicts as barriers, see them as mirrors that reflect our emotions, needs, and values. Disagreements often arise because there is something important at stake for both parties. Recognizing this importance is the first step in turning conflict into a constructive conversation. By doing so, we shift the focus from "win or lose" to "understand and resolve." And in that change, we not only find solutions; We build trust and respect.

Transforming conflicts also requires humility and empathy. It is accepting that our perspectives are not the only valid ones, and that the other has a story and a purpose that deserves to be heard.

By asking sincerely: *"What do you need from this situation? How can we work together to solve this?"*, we create a space where differences become opportunities to innovate and collaborate.

What relationships could you strengthen today if you chose to ask more and assume less?

Harriet Tubman is a timeless example of how authentic and courageous leadership can emerge in the darkest of times. Born into slavery in 1822, Tubman not only escaped her own oppression, but became a beacon of hope for hundreds of people seeking freedom. In times of crisis, when fear and uncertainty paralyzed many, she rose as a leader, guiding others with unwavering determination and a heart full of empathy.

Tubman led with action, not just words. For more than a decade, she worked tirelessly as a "conductor" on the Underground Railroad, a secret network that helped slaves escape to freedom in the North.

On each journey, she faced unimaginable dangers: bounty hunters, oppressive laws, and a hostile environment. However, she was never intimidated.

Tubman understood that true leadership in times of crisis required making bold decisions, even when the risk was immense.

What made Harriet Tubman an extraordinary leader was not only her bravery, but also her empathy. Each person she helped escape was not just a number; It was a life she deeply valued. Tubman made sure each member of her group felt safe and supported, even in the most critical moments.

She knew the fear they faced, because she had felt it herself, and she used that understanding motivating them to keep going. In her own words:

> *"I've crossed that line. I've looked back and seen the smiling faces, and oh, what a joy it was to see them."*

Her leadership was not only strategic, but deeply human. Harriet Tubman knew that leading meant much more than guiding people to a physical destination; It meant inspiring them to believe in a better future.

Known as "Moses," she not only freed hundreds of people, but also lit a flame of hope in thousands more. Through her example, she demonstrated that even in the most difficult circumstances, one committed person can make a monumental difference.

Tubman did not stop with the abolition of slavery. During the Civil War, she worked as a nurse, spy, and strategist for the Union Army, risking her life once again to fight for freedom and justice. Her ability to lead in the midst of chaos not only changed lives, but helped change the course of history.

Harriet Tubman's legacy inspires us to face our own crises with courage and compassion. It teaches us that even when the path seems impossible, authentic leadership can light the way for others.

Her life is a reminder that leading is not about waiting for challenges to go away, but about facing them with a clear purpose and a heart full of empathy.

How can you lead in times of crisis?

Maybe the first step is to look inward, find your purpose, and decide that, like Harriet Tubman, you will never stop moving forward.

> *"Whenever I enter a place, I know I'm going to get out of it successfully."*
> -Harriet Tubman-

In the most difficult times, conflict can teach us something invaluable about ourselves. They challenge us to be patient, to manage our emotions, and to respond with integrity. Every disagreement is an opportunity to demonstrate who we really are and what values we choose to prioritize.

Are you going to let the conflict define you, or will you define it?

Possibly it's time to lead from a place of calm, looking for solutions instead of blame.

In the end, transforming conflicts into opportunities not only benefits others; It also enriches us. It allows us to grow as leaders, as friends, as colleagues and as human beings. Each conflict resolved with empathy and determination leaves a mark, not only on the relationship, but also on our ability to face future challenges with more wisdom.

So today, instead of fearing the next conflict, see it as a door. Open it with confidence, and you may find not just a solution, but an opportunity to build something stronger, more meaningful, and more lasting. Because in conflicts there is no end; is the beginning of something new.

Practical Strategies to Resolve Conflicts

Active Listening: Take time to understand the perspectives of all parties. Ask open-ended questions and validate their emotions.

- Example: In a meeting, give space for each person to explain their point of view without interruptions.

Find Common Interests: Instead of focusing on differences, identify shared goals that can serve as the basis for a resolution.

- Example: If there is a conflict in a team, focus the discussion on how to achieve collective goals.

Practice Impartiality: Maintain a neutral position and avoid taking sides. Facilitates dialogue so that the parties find equitable solutions.

- Example: Act as a mediator, making sure all voices are heard.

Practical Exercise: Turning Conflict into a Bridge for Growth

Conflicts are not obstacles—they are gateways.

Gateways that, when opened with awareness and respect, can lead us to deeper understanding, more authentic relationships, and personal growth.

This exercise invites you to see conflict not as something to avoid, but as an opportunity to build, heal, and lead with wisdom.

---

1. Identify a Current Conflict and Observe It Clearly

Think of a recent disagreement—whether in your personal life or professional environment.
Maybe it was an uncomfortable conversation, an unresolved tension, or a clash of perspectives that still lingers beneath the surface.

Now, without judgment, observe:

- What did you feel during the conflict?

- What do you believe the other person was feeling?

- What needs were being expressed—either clearly or indirectly—by both sides?

Write down each person's perspective as if you were a neutral observer. This will help you move from judgment to understanding.

---

2. Explore Creative Solutions with Emotional Awareness

Not every conflict has a perfect solution, but almost all can be transformed when approached with creativity and empathy.

Brainstorm at least three different ways you could address this situation. Ask yourself:

- What options might allow both people to feel heard and valued?

- How can I shift the energy from confrontation to collaboration?

- Is there common ground we may have overlooked?

Emotional awareness is key.
This is not just about solving a problem—it's about **preserving the relationship** while doing so.

---

3. Choose One Action and Apply It with Empathy

Select the solution that feels most balanced and aligned with your values.
Now, take action—with presence, humility, and openness.

When speaking with the other person:

- Use language that invites rather than confronts.

- Speak from your own experience (*"I felt..."*) instead of blaming (*"You did..."*).

- Listen as much as you speak.

- Acknowledge the validity of their perspective, even if you don't fully agree with it.

Acting with empathy doesn't mean giving in—it means choosing resolution over resistance, and connection over control.

Final Reflection: The Power to Heal Through Conflict

After completing this exercise, take a moment to reflect:

- What did I learn about myself through this situation?

- What did I learn about the other person?

- How can I apply this experience to grow as a leader and as a human being?

Remember:
Leaders are not defined by their ability to avoid conflict, but by how they navigate it.

With empathy, listening, and awareness, every conflict can become a bridge toward a stronger, more meaningful connection.

Chapter 5:

From Friends to Allies in Leadership

Effective leadership does not occur in isolation; It is built through meaningful relationships that evolve from sincere friendships to strategic alliances. Think for a moment: how many of your current friendships could be transformed into collaborations that leave a lasting impact? What are you doing today to strengthen those relationships and turn them into allies that help you achieve your goals and dreams?

This chapter explores the keys to transforming friendships into productive, lasting collaborations, highlighting inspiring examples and practical strategies.

The Evolution of Relationships: From Personal Connections to Professional Alliances

Great alliances do not begin as strategic agreements; They begin as authentic human connections. A sincere friendship, a bond of trust, or even a gesture of support at the right time can be the starting point for a collaboration that transcends the personal and generates a lasting professional impact. Relationships not only transform over time; They evolve when both parties choose to invest in them with intention and purpose.

How many of your personal connections could become something more meaningful if you gave them the space to flourish?

The key to this evolution is trust. Personal connections, like friendships, are built on empathy and mutual respect. When we translate those values into a professional relationship, we create fertile ground for collaboration. It is not just about sharing goals, but about sharing principles, dreams and a common vision.

Consider the following:

Who in your life shares your values and could be your ally in a larger project?

Maybe You already have that person close, waiting for you to recognize their potential.

Successful professional alliances do not eliminate the personal; they integrate it. A relationship that evolves into productive collaboration does not leave human connection behind, but rather reinforces it. It is that connection that means differences are handled with respect and challenges are faced with a team spirit.

Knowing that you have someone by your side who understands both your strengths and weaknesses creates an unbreakable foundation for working together toward a greater goal.

This evolution also requires open communication and role clarity. In a professional environment, expectations should be clearly defined to avoid misunderstandings and unnecessary conflict. But beyond responsibilities, what really sustains an alliance is the willingness of both to adapt and grow together. An alliance is not only based on what you can get, but on what you can contribute to strengthen the relationship.

What are you doing today to nurture your personal and professional connections?

When a personal connection transforms into a professional alliance, not only goals are achieved; legacies are created. These relationships have the power to change not only your life, but also the lives of the people around you. Because when you work with someone who understands your vision, you're not building something separately; you are building something together, something that transcends.

In the end, the evolution of relationships is a reminder that human connections are the foundation of any meaningful achievement. How can you transform the connections in your life into alliances that impact beyond the individual? Maybe it all starts with an honest conversation, an act of trust, or a shared dream. Because in every authentic relationship, there is infinite potential waiting to be discovered.

Are you ready to take that step?

Building Alliances Based on Shared Values

The strongest alliances are not forged just around common goals, but on shared values. Those principles that guide our decisions, our actions, and our worldviews are the foundation that sustains any meaningful collaboration. Building alliances based on shared values not only ensures joint direction, but also creates a bond of trust and purpose that can withstand the toughest challenges.

How many of your current relationships are built on something deeper than superficial interests?

A shared value is more than an idea; It is a compass that defines how people act, both in moments of success and in times of adversity. When you find someone who shares your values, you're not just working with that person; you are aligning your efforts with a larger vision. This connection generates a synchronicity that drives creativity, innovation and resilience, because both know that they are committed to something that transcends immediate results.

To build alliances based on shared values, you first need clarity about your own values.

What do you value most in a collaboration? Integrity, creativity, respect, commitment?

By defining your principles, you can more easily identify the people who share your vision and with whom you can build something lasting.

Take a moment to reflect and ask yourself:

Are my current relationships aligned with the values I consider core?

Maybe This is the time to strengthen those connections or seek new alliances.

Open communication is key in these alliances. Sharing your values and listening to the other people establishes common ground from the start. This transparency not only strengthens trust, but also avoids misunderstandings that may arise along the way. When both know that they are guided by similar principles, decisions are made more easily and differences are handled with respect.

Partnerships based on shared values not only benefit the individuals involved; They also have the power to positively influence their environment. These partnerships inspire others and create an impact that transcends the professional, leaving a legacy of collaboration and purpose.

Building alliances based on shared values takes time, effort and authenticity, but the result is worth it. These relationships not only achieve results; They enrich our lives and connect us to something bigger than ourselves.

So today, reflect on your values and find people who share them. Because when we work with those who share our convictions, we not only move forward; We build something that can change the world.

What alliance could you start today that is based on what really matters?

Overcoming Challenges in Professional Relationships

Professional relationships, like personal ones, are full of challenges. Differences of opinion, misunderstandings, conflicts of interest and unmet expectations are inevitable in any work environment. But it is precisely in those moments of difficulty where relationships have the opportunity to strengthen.

Overcoming challenges does not mean avoiding them, but facing them with courage, empathy, and a solution mindset.

How many times has well-handled conflict led to a stronger relationship and deeper understanding?

The first step to overcoming any professional challenge is open and honest communication. Many times, problems are not as big as they seem; they simply have not been addressed effectively. Speaking from a place of respect and clarity, without blame or blame, opens the door to understanding.

When was the last time you sat down to talk with someone with whom you had a disagreement?

Perhaps you would discover that you are both looking for the same thing, just from different angles.

Empathy also plays a crucial role. Instead of assuming negative intentions, stop and consider asking yourself:

What could this person be feeling or facing that I'm not seeing?

Often, challenges arise not from a lack of will, but from a lack of understanding. Putting yourself in someone else's shoes not only defuses tensions, but also builds trust and mutual respect. This simple act can transform a confrontational environment into one of collaboration.

Another essential component is flexibility. Successful professional relationships are not built on rigidity, but on the ability to adapt and compromise. This does not mean giving in on everything, but rather finding solutions that benefit both parties.

What could you achieve if you allowed yourself to be more flexible in your approach?

Sometimes a small concession can be the catalyst to solving big challenges.

Finally, overcoming challenges requires patience and perseverance. Not all solutions come immediately, and some relationships take time to heal.

Recognize that challenges are part of the process and that facing them together, rather than avoiding them, strengthens the professional bond. Every problem overcome is an opportunity to demonstrate resilience, commitment, and the value of working as a team.

Eleanor Roosevelt y Mary McLeod Bethune They forged one of the most influential alliances of the 20th century, based on their shared vision of social justice and civil rights. However, their relationship was not without challenges, especially at a time when racial and gender divisions were deeply entrenched.

Their ability to overcome these barriers and build an authentic and powerful professional connection is a shining example of how facing challenges can strengthen and transform a relationship.

When they met, Eleanor Roosevelt was the First Lady of the United States, a white woman in a position of privilege who was beginning to become interested in social justice. Mary McLeod Bethune, on the other hand, was an African American educator and activist who fought against racial inequality and worked to empower her community in a context of extreme segregation.

Despite their differences in origin, both shared a deep commitment to human rights, which united them in a common mission.

One of the biggest challenges they faced was public perception. At a time when relationships between black and white women were viewed with disdain by many, their friendship and professional collaboration challenged social norms. Instead of allowing these tensions to tear them apart, they used criticism as an opportunity to educate and create change.

Eleanor, aware of her position of privilege, humbly listened and learned from Mary's experience and wisdom, while Mary, with patience and determination, helped Eleanor understand the complexities of the civil rights struggle.

Together they faced institutional challenges by advancing initiatives such as the creation of the Division of Black Affairs in the National Youth Administration (NYA). This program provided employment and educational opportunities to young African Americans, marking a milestone in social inclusion. To achieve this, they had to overcome the resistance of political and social leaders who opposed these reforms.

Their ability to work together, despite external pressures, demonstrated that a professional relationship based on respect and shared values can achieve the impossible.

The relationship between Eleanor and Mary not only had a political impact, but also a personal one. Through their collaboration, both women grew as leaders and as people. Eleanor became a more vocal advocate for civil rights, while Mary expanded her reach and influence by working closely with the White House.

Together, they showed the world that challenges are not obstacles, but opportunities to demonstrate leadership, empathy, and commitment.

Their legacy inspires us to see challenges in professional relationships as catalysts for change. Like Eleanor and Mary, we can choose to face tensions with openness, learn from differences, and work together toward a greater purpose. Because when we overcome challenges in a professional relationship, we not only achieve our goals; We also build an impact that can transcend generations.

What could you achieve today if you decided to face a challenge with the same courage and collaboration as these two visionary leaders?

"Faith is the greatest antidote to failure. Believe in yourself and others."
-Mary McLeod Bethune-

Overcoming challenges in professional relationships not only resolves conflicts; It also generates personal and professional growth. It is in these difficult times when we show who we really are and build a reputation based on integrity and leadership.

So the next time you face a challenge in a professional relationship, see it as an opportunity to learn, connect, and strengthen. Because in every obstacle there is a lesson, and in every relationship there is infinite potential waiting to be discovered.

What challenge could you transform today into an opportunity?

Practical Exercise: Transforming Friendships into Purposeful Alliances

The greatest success stories are rarely written in solitude.
More often than not, our real momentum toward our goals comes from those who walk beside us.

This exercise invites you to see your friendships through a new lens—not just as emotional bonds, but as fertile ground for powerful, intentional alliances that foster creation, impact, and shared growth.

---

1. Identify a Friendship with Collaborative Potential

Think of someone close to you—someone with whom you share more than affection:

- Do you have aligned values, similar passions, or intersecting dreams?

- Is there a dynamic of mutual respect, admiration, or inspiration?

Visualize this relationship not just as a friendship, but as a space with the potential to **co-create**.
Ask yourself:

- *What could we build together that feels meaningful?*
- *What strengths do each of us bring to the table?*
- *What would it take to elevate this connection into something purposeful?*

This first step is about recognizing that deep connections can also become powerful engines of collaboration.

---

2. Establish a Shared Purpose

Every meaningful alliance is rooted in a common vision.
Initiate a conversation from a place of curiosity and possibility. You don't need to have it all figured out—just explore the terrain together.

Invite them into a dialogue where you can dream out loud:

- *What could we do together that lights us both up?*
- *How might we collaborate on something that adds value to others or to our community?*
- *What kind of impact could we create by combining our talents and passions?*

This conversation doesn't have to be formal—let it happen over a walk, a cup of coffee, or a deep video call.
The key is to plant a seed *together*.

3. Design a Conscious Action Plan

Great alliances don't just dream—they move.
Once you've defined your shared purpose, take the next step by structuring a simple but clear plan:

- Who will take on which roles?

- What will the first steps look like?

- What timeline will you follow that allows for flow, not pressure?

Defining expectations early prevents misunderstandings and strengthens mutual commitment.
Remember: a true alliance is a dance of reciprocity—not a burden carried alone.

Final Reflection: When Friendship Becomes a Creative Force

After completing this exercise, take a moment to reflect:

- How did the energy between you shift after speaking from a place of purpose?

- What did it feel like to imagine a friendship that also builds, creates, and uplifts?

- What part of you expanded as you moved from *"me"* to *"we"*?

Friendships that evolve into alliances remind us that shared success isn't just more possible—it's more fulfilling.

Remember: an authentic alliance doesn't just multiply outcomes. It multiplies meaning.

Chapter 6:

The Power of Authentic Communication

Authentic communication is the bridge that connects our ideas, emotions, and values with others. It is not just about words, but about intentions and actions that generate trust, strengthen bonds and mobilize people towards a common purpose. In this chapter, we will explore how to master this essential skill to become an inspiring and transformative leader.

The Essence of Authentic Communication

Authentic communication is the lifeblood of any meaningful relationship. It's not just about transmitting information, but about creating a genuine connection based on honesty, vulnerability, and respect.

In a world where words are often used to impress or convince, speaking from the heart has become an act of courage. Authenticity in communication not only strengthens bonds, but also allows us to be seen and understood as we are.

> **How many times have you wished that someone would speak to you with complete sincerity?**

That connection is the gift that authentic communication can offer.

Speaking authentically means expressing what we really think and feel, without masks or unnecessary embellishments. But it also means doing it with empathy, taking into account the other person's emotions and perspectives. This balance between honesty and thoughtfulness creates a space where conversations not only inform, but transform.

Authentic communication is not afraid of uncomfortable truths, but approaches them with respect and sensitivity.

Reflect for a moment:

How would your relationships change if you chose to be completely honest in your words?

Authenticity also lies in listening with intention. It's not just about waiting your turn to speak, but about absorbing what the other person says, capturing the nuances and emotions behind their words. Listening in this way creates fertile ground for mutual understanding. Through active listening, we show that we value not just what someone says, but who they are as a person.

When was the last time you really listened to someone, putting aside your own ideas and judgments?

Maybe it's time to practice that level of presence.

Nelson Mandela, an iconic leader and symbol of the fight for freedom, possessed an exceptional ability to communicate with clarity, empathy, and purpose. His way of speaking not only inspired, but also united people of diverse backgrounds and perspectives.

Mandela understood that words have the power to heal wounds, break down barriers and build bridges, even in the darkest moments. His life and legacy are a living example of how authentic communication can transform conflicts into opportunities and enemies into allies.

Mandela spent 27 years in prison, but even in that isolation, he honed his ability to listen and communicate. He knew that if he ever achieved freedom, he would need to speak with a voice that united, not divided.

When he was finally released in 1990, his first speech was neither a declaration of revenge nor recrimination, but a call for reconciliation.

Addressing both the oppressed and the oppressors, Mandela said:

> *"We must forget our differences and unite as one people."*

These words not only calmed tensions, but set the tone for South Africa's peaceful transition to democracy.

One of the keys to his ability to communicate was his ability to actively listen. Mandela not only spoke to be heard, but also took the time to understand the perspectives of others, even those with whom he disagreed.

During negotiations to dismantle apartheid, Mandela insisted on sitting down with his bitterest enemies, not to confront them, but to understand them. He knew that only by acknowledging the fears and motivations of all parties could he build lasting peace.

Mandela also used stories to convey his messages in a way that resonated deeply with his audience. He knew that people not only remember facts, but also emotions. For example, in his inaugural address as president in 1994, he shared a vision of hope and unity, reminding South Africans that the country could overcome its painful past if they worked together.

His words were not just political speeches; they were calls to action that connected people to a greater purpose.

Furthermore, Mandela showed that body language and tone are as important as words. His calm posture, measured voice, and willingness to smile even in tense moments sent a clear message: He was there to unite, not divide. These qualities made him a magnetic communicator, able to inspire trust and respect even among his critics.

Nelson Mandela's ability to communicate not only transformed South Africa, but also inspired the world. He taught us that true communication is not just talking; It is listening, connecting, and leading with the heart.

He used his voice not to amplify divisions, but to build a path toward reconciliation and unity. His legacy invites us to reflect:

How can you use your voice to inspire, unite and transform?

Because, as Mandela demonstrated, when we communicate with empathy and purpose, we can change not only conversations, but the course of history.

Authentic communication is a powerful tool for resolving conflict and strengthening relationships. When we are open and vulnerable, we invite others to do the same, creating a circle of trust.

This not only improves the quality of our interactions, but also fosters a culture of transparency and collaboration. At work, in family, or among friends, speaking from a place of authenticity allows us to address challenges with clarity and find solutions that benefit everyone.

But being authentic in communication also requires courage. It means accepting that we will not always be understood or that our words may not be well received. Even so, authenticity frees us from the burden of appearances and allows us to build relationships on solid and real foundations. It is an act of love towards ourselves and towards others, because only when we are authentic can we experience true connections.

The essence of authentic communication is in its ability to unite. It is a reminder that behind every word, there is a heart, a mind and a story. So the next time you talk, ask yourself:

Am I being genuine? Am I listening with an open heart?

You may find that authenticity not only improves your conversations, but also your relationships and your life. Because, in the end, authentic words not only inform; They inspire, connect and transform.

What impact could you have if you chose to communicate with complete authenticity?

Listen to Connect

Listening is much more than hearing words; It is an act of deep human connection. In a world full of noise, where everyone wants to be heard, but few are really paying attention, the skill of listening becomes a powerful bridge to meaningful relationships. Listening to connect is not just a polite gesture; It is a gift you give to the other person, a silent message that says: *"I see you, I hear you, you matter."*

How many times in your life have you longed for that kind of mindfulness?

Now imagine being the one who offers it.

When you listen to connect, you are creating a space where emotions can flow freely and barriers disappear. It's not about preparing your response while the other person speaks, but about being completely present, focused on what the other person is saying, how they are saying it, and what is behind their words. This type of listening not only strengthens bonds, but also fosters trust and mutual understanding.

I want to ask you:

When was the last time you listened with an open heart, without interruptions or judgment?

The connection that comes from active listening is transformative. It allows us to capture not only the words, but also the feelings, concerns, and dreams of the other person. It's as if, for a moment, you share their world, seeing things from their perspective. This empathy not only improves the quality of interaction, but also enriches us as individuals, expanding our ability to understand and relate to others.

Oprah Winfrey is a shining example of how the act of listening can become a transformative tool for building deep and meaningful connections.

As one of the most influential figures in media, Oprah has not only interviewed thousands of people, from celebrities to everyday citizens, but she has created a unique space where stories are told authentically and emotions are shared without fear.

Your success lies not only in your ability to ask questions, but in your ability to listen with genuine attention and empathy.

In each interview, Oprah demonstrates that listening is not just picking up words, but understanding the heart behind them. When someone sits across from her, no matter how famous or unknown, they feel like they are truly being heard.

In several of her interviews, she has mentioned that one of the most common phrases she hears is: *"I felt so comfortable talking to you, like you understood me completely."* That feeling of connection is a result of your ability to listen without interruptions or judgment.

A moment that encapsulates his ability to listen to connect occurred during her interview with Viola Davis. In that conversation, Davis talked about her childhood struggles, her insecurity, and her path to success.

Oprah not only heard Davis' words, she caught the emotions behind them. Through her body language, her thoughtful responses, and her ability to ask questions that showed deep understanding, she helped Davis open up even more, creating a moment of authenticity that resonated with millions of viewers.

Oprah's ability to listen has also allowed her to connect with her audience on a deep level. When you share stories or reflect on your guests' experiences, you show that you have captured not only the details, but also the emotional essence of what has been shared. This approach not only enriches her interviews, but also inspires her audience to reflect on their own lives and relationships.

Think about it for a moment:

What impact could it have on your life and the lives of others if you chose to listen with that level of attentiveness and empathy?

Beyond interviews, Oprah has used her platform to amplify the voices of those who often go unheard. Her commitment to listening to connect has led her to promote social causes, support marginalized communities, and make space for stories that inspire and educate.

This approach has not only solidified her legacy, but has also demonstrated that the power of listening can transcend individual conversations and create a global impact.

Oprah Winfrey teaches us that listening is not just a skill, but an act of love and respect. Her life is a reminder that when we listen with intention and empathy, we not only connect with others, but we also give them the gift of feeling seen and valued.

So the next time you have the chance to listen, do it like Oprah: with an open heart, with genuine curiosity, and with the intention to connect. Because by listening to connect, you transform not only your relationships, but also the world around you.

> *"We all want to be heard and understood. It is the greatest gift we can give each other."*
> -Oprah Winfrey-

Listening to connect also means letting go of our own agendas and truly putting the other person first. It is an act of generosity that takes us out of ourselves and leads us to focus completely on the other.

In a society where speed and multitasking are the norm, choosing to listen with intention is a declaration that we value relationships more than distractions.

What impact could you have on your relationships if you took a moment to listen, not to respond, but to understand?

In the end, listening to connect not only benefits those we listen to, but also ourselves. It gives us the gift of authentic connection, that feeling of being part of something bigger than ourselves. It reminds us that, behind every voice, there is a story, an emotion, and a humanity that deserves to be recognized. So the next time someone talks to you, stop, listen and connect.

Because when listening, you don't just hear words; you build bridges, break barriers and create a space where understanding can flourish.

Are you ready to listen with an open heart?

Today will be the day to start.

Vulnerability as Strength

Vulnerability, often misinterpreted as a sign of weakness, is actually one of the greatest strengths we can possess. It is the courage to show ourselves as we are: imperfect, human, real. Being vulnerable does not mean exposing ourselves without limits, but rather allowing ourselves to be authentic, even when there is the risk of being misunderstood or rejected.

In a world that prizes appearances and invulnerability, choosing vulnerability is an act of profound courage.

How many times have you felt immense relief when sharing your truth with someone?

That is the transformative power of being authentic.

Vulnerability is not an obstacle to connections; It is the bridge that makes them possible. When we allow ourselves to be open, we show others that we trust them and give them permission to do the same. This genuine exchange creates deeper, more meaningful relationships. Instead of hiding our struggles, by sharing them we allow others to see that they are not alone in their own battles.

So ask yourself:

What impact could it have on my relationships if I chose to be a little more vulnerable today?

In leadership, vulnerability is a powerful tool. Admitting that you don't have all the answers, sharing your learnings from failures, and showing empathy toward others does not diminish your authority; reinforces it. A leader who embraces vulnerability inspires not because he is perfect, but because he is real. This type of leadership builds trust and fosters a culture where people feel safe to be authentic, innovate, and learn from their mistakes.

How could you lead from vulnerability in your environment?

Vulnerability also connects us to our shared humanity. It reminds us that we all face fears, insecurities and challenges. By embracing our own vulnerabilities, we become more compassionate toward those of others.

This act of acceptance not only strengthens our relationships, but also frees us from the pressure of perfection, allowing us to live with greater authenticity and inner peace.

Brené Brown, renowned researcher, author and speaker, has dedicated her career to exploring the power of vulnerability and how this, far from being a weakness, is one of the most transformative strengths we can embrace.

Her work has changed the global perception of what it means to be vulnerable, challenging the idea that we must hide our imperfections to be strong.

Through her research and personal experiences, Brené shows us that vulnerability is the heart of connection, the engine of courage, and the key to living an authentic life.

Brown began her professional journey studying topics such as shame and human connection. What she discovered was revealing: the happiest and most fulfilled people were not those who avoided vulnerability, but those who embraced it.

These people were not afraid to show their emotions, admit their mistakes or share their fears. Instead, they saw vulnerability as a way to be genuine and establish deeper relationships. This finding challenged traditional beliefs about strength and became the basis for her influential TED talk, **The power of vulnerability**, which has been viewed by millions of people around the world.

In that talk, Brown shared her own journey toward accepting vulnerability. She talked about how, for a long time, she tried to control and perfect every aspect of her life to avoid the pain and discomfort of being seen as she was. However, this approach led to emotional exhaustion and disconnection.

It was only when she allowed herself to be vulnerable that she discovered the true power of living authentically. Her words resonated deeply with her audience because they reflected a universal truth: *we all want to be seen and accepted as we are.*

Brown's work also highlights how vulnerability is fundamental to leadership. In her book, *Dare to Lead* argues that the best leaders are not those who project perfection, but rather those who dare to be human.

A leader who admits their limitations and shares their struggles inspires confidence and fosters a work environment where people feel safe to innovate, learn, and collaborate. According to Brown, leading from vulnerability is not a sign of weakness, but rather a demonstration of courage and strength.

Brené Brown reminds us that vulnerability is not optional; It is part of the human experience. What matters is how we choose to respond to it. We can see it as a risk or as an opportunity to connect, grow and live with purpose.

By sharing her story and research, Brown invites us to change our relationship with vulnerability and see it as a powerful tool for building a fuller, more meaningful life.

Her legacy inspires us to embrace our imperfections and show the world who we really are, with all that that entails. By doing so, we not only connect more deeply with others, but also with ourselves.

So today, reflect:

What might change in your life if you chose to see vulnerability as a strength instead of a weakness?

Perhaps, like Brené Brown, you will discover that in your vulnerability lies the power to transform not only your relationships, but also your history.

> *"Vulnerability is not weakness; it is our most accurate measure of courage."*
> -Brené Brown-

Beyond relationships, vulnerability is key to personal growth. It is the engine that drives us to take risks, pursue dreams and face the fear of failure. Every time we choose to be vulnerable, we are saying: *"'I am strong enough to be seen for who I am."*

It is through this courage that we discover our true potential and open the door to opportunities that previously seemed unattainable to us.

Ultimately, vulnerability is not a burden; It is a strength that allows us to connect, lead and grow. So today, take a step into your vulnerability. Share a truth, ask for help, or simply allow yourself to feel. Because by showing yourself as you are, you not only inspire others to do the same, but you also discover the power that lies in embracing your authenticity.

Are you ready to transform your vulnerability into your greatest strength?

Maybe, in that act of courage, you will find the connection and purpose you have been searching for.

Practical Strategies for Authentic Communication

Speak from the Heart: Share your ideas and emotions honestly, but always with respect.

o Example: In a difficult conversation, explain how you feel instead of blaming or criticizing.

Listen with Empathy: Spend time actively listening to others, asking open-ended questions and showing genuine interest.

o Example: During a meeting, focus completely on what the other person is saying, without interrupting or thinking about your response.

Adapt your Message to your Audience: Authenticity does not mean communicating the same with everyone. Consider the needs and perspectives of those listening to you.

o Example: Use clear, accessible language when explaining a complex topic to someone who is not familiar with it.

Practical Exercise: Elevating Your Communication Through Authenticity

Communication is not just about delivering information.
It's about revealing who you are, connecting from the soul, and creating spaces where truth can be spoken—and received—with respect.

This exercise will help you align your communication with your essence, strengthening your ability to influence, inspire, and connect from a place of truth.

1. Reflect Honestly on Your Communication Style

Pause for a moment and observe yourself with kindness:

- How do you tend to express yourself under pressure?

- What emotions usually guide your communication—fear, clarity, empathy, defensiveness?

- Are your tone, words, and body language aligned with your core values?

Take out a notebook and create two columns:
Strengths — aspects of your communication that feel authentic, clear, or empathetic.
Areas to improve — patterns that may be limiting your connections (like interrupting, being defensive, or avoiding difficult conversations).

Ask yourself:

Is my communication building bridges… or creating walls?

2. Practice Active Listening as a Form of Presence

Devote an entire day to becoming a conscious listener.
In every conversation, make the commitment not to interrupt.
Rather than thinking about your response, focus on *understanding*.

Notice:

- What emotions lie beneath the other person's words?

- What does their body language reveal beyond what is spoken?

- How does the dynamic shift when you simply listen without trying to fix or reply?

Active listening doesn't just transform others—it transforms *you*.
Because when you listen from the soul, the other person feels safe to be fully seen.

3. Share a Personal Story with Intention

In your next meaningful conversation or team meeting, choose to share something personal:

- A challenge that taught you a powerful lesson.

- A mistake that helped you grow.

- An experience that ties into the message you want to convey.

This isn't about taking the spotlight—it's about *bringing your humanity into the room*.
When shared with purpose, vulnerability has the power to open hearts and build deep trust.

Afterward, observe:

- How did the energy in the space shift?

- What impact did your openness have on others?

Final Reflection: Communicating to Connect, Not Just to Be Heard

As you close this exercise, ask yourself:

- What did I feel when I listened more intentionally?

- What did I learn about myself by observing the way I speak?

- How did my view of communication change when I used it to serve connection, not control?

Remember: authentic communication is a quiet form of leadership.
It doesn't impose. It doesn't shout.

It invites. It opens. It unites.

And when you cultivate it, you don't just transform your relationships—

You become a leader who speaks with soul and leaves a lasting mark.

Chapter 7:

How to Make Others Follow You

Effective leadership is not imposed; it is inspired. Getting others to follow you is not about manipulation or control, but about building trust, building a shared vision, and acting with integrity. Think about a time when you decided to follow someone. What inspired you? His/her clarity, his/her passion, his/her example? In this chapter, we'll explore how you can become the kind of leader that people choose to follow, not because they have to, but because they want to.

The Importance of Inspiration

Inspiration is the fire that lights the soul and moves people to dream, believe and act. It is not something superficial or temporary; It is a profound force that has the power to transform lives and open doors to the extraordinary. Inspiration not only drives us to achieve our goals, but also connects us to a larger purpose. It is that moment when we feel that anything is possible, that our actions have meaning and that we can make a difference in the world.

> **How many times has a spark of inspiration led you to make a decision that changed your life?**

Inspiration is contagious. When a person acts motivated by a clear vision and genuine purpose, they become a source of energy to those around them. It is like lighting a candle that can illuminate others without losing its own light. Whether in a work team, a family, or a community, inspiration has the power to unite people towards a common goal, awakening their creativity and passion.

I want you to analyze it for a moment:

What could you achieve if you chose to inspire others with your actions and your words?

Florence Nightingale, known as "The Lady with the Lamp," not only revolutionized healthcare, but inspired generations through her vision, determination, and humanity. At a time when nursing was not considered a respectable profession, Nightingale transformed this perception and set standards that saved countless lives. Her ability to inspire was not solely in her actions, but in her ability to motivate others to believe in a greater purpose: caring for the sick with dignity, compassion, and science.

During the Crimean War (1853-1856), Nightingale faced bleak conditions in military hospitals, where filth, lack of organization, and infections killed more soldiers than battle wounds themselves. Armed with a deep sense of purpose and innovative knowledge of hygiene and public health, she not only oversaw the cleanliness of hospitals, but also introduced practices that dramatically reduced mortality rates. Her work was not easy; She faced resistance from officers and doctors who did not want to change their methods. However, her example and leadership calmed fears and gained allies.

What made Nightingale extraordinary was not only her ability to lead effectively, but her ability to inspire confidence and hope in those around her. The wounded soldiers would see her walking through the hallways with her lamp at night, checking them out one by one. This simple but compassionate act earned her the nickname "The Lady with the Lamp" and became a symbol of care and dedication. Men who were once hopeless felt comforted, knowing that someone really cared about them.

Think for a moment:

What impact could you have on someone's life simply by showing empathy and commitment?

Nightingale not only transformed caring on the battlefield, she also dedicated her life to establishing nursing as a respected, science-based profession. She founded the first formal nursing school in 1860, where she promoted rigorous standards and a patient-centered approach. Her writings, especially *Notes on Nursing*, they not only educated nurses, but also inspired entire communities to prioritize hygiene and public health. Nightingale didn't just offer solutions; empowered others to act.

What was most notable about Florence Nightingale was her ability to lead with a clear vision, even in the midst of adversity. She inspired not only the soldiers she cared for, but also governments, doctors, and society at large, demonstrating that positive change is possible with determination and humanity. Her legacy not only changed the course of healthcare history, but continues to motivate millions in the field of nursing and public health.

The story of Florence Nightingale reminds us that inspiration can be born even in the most difficult circumstances. Her life is an example of how one person, guided by a clear purpose, can transform not only a system, but also the lives of those around him/her. So the next time you face a challenge, ask yourself:

How can I inspire others with my actions?

Perhaps, like Nightingale, you will discover that even the simplest gestures can light a flame of hope and change in the world.

> *"I attribute my success to this: I never gave or accepted any excuses."*
> -Florence Nightingale-

Being a source of inspiration does not require being perfect or having all the answers; It requires authenticity and courage. The most inspiring stories are those of people who, despite their challenges, chose to move forward with courage and purpose. By sharing our experiences, both victories and struggles, we show others that they too can overcome their obstacles and achieve their dreams. In the end, inspiration is not about impressing, but empowering.

Inspiration also reminds us that we are capable of more than we think. It's that reminder that even in the darkest moments, there is something within us that can rise and shine. When we are inspired, we not only see our goals more clearly, but we also find the energy and determination to pursue them. It connects us with our best version, the one that is willing to make an effort, learn and grow.

Ultimately, inspiration transcends individual actions; It is a force that changes realities. When you choose to inspire, you are creating an impact that can last far beyond your words or actions. You are planting seeds of hope and transformation in the people around you. So today, decide to be a source of inspiration. Share your story, pursue your dreams and live with purpose. Because, as you know, inspiration doesn't just change lives; It transforms them completely.

What will you do today to inspire someone else?

That is where the spark that will ignite something extraordinary will be found.

The Battle of May 5th: Ignacio Zaragoza and His Power To Inspire To Others

It was May 5, 1862. On the hills of Loreto and Guadalupe, in Puebla, Mexico, a poorly armed army—mostly made up of farmers, indigenous people, and everyday citizens—stood ready to face one of the most powerful military forces in the world: the French army. Under the rain, wearing mismatched uniforms, with little formal military training and uncertainty hanging heavy in the air, these men weren't held together by the strength of their weapons, but by something far deeper: **the conviction of being led by a man who believed in them more than they believed in themselves.**

That man was **General Ignacio Zaragoza**. A young leader, with a calm yet firm voice, who didn't inspire by barking orders, but by walking in front—dignified and humble—reminding every soldier that they weren't just defending land, but **honor, freedom, and the very**

soul of their nation.

Zaragoza understood that a true leader doesn't need greatness to be followed—but purpose. And that day, instead of focusing on the odds stacked against them or the might of the enemy, he chose to focus on the courage of the Mexican heart. He walked through the camps, looked his men in the eyes, and spoke with a simplicity that shattered fear:

"Our enemies are the first soldiers of the world, but you are the first sons of Mexico."

He didn't promise easy victories, but he made it clear they would fight with dignity. And that was enough. Because a leader who **speaks with truth, passion, and purpose** doesn't need to persuade—he only needs to ignite the spirit of his people.

The result was historic. That day, Mexico didn't just win a battle against the world's most feared army—it won something even greater: **the certainty that when people believe in themselves and their cause, no empire is invincible.**

Zaragoza left us with a timeless lesson: people don't follow the loudest voice or the one with the most power. They follow the one with a clear vision, the one who walks beside them, the one who reminds them who they are and what they are capable of. They follow the leader who **makes them feel part of something greater than themselves.**

So pause for a moment and reflect:

Are you leading by example?

Are you inspiring with purpose?

You may not be on a battlefield, but each day is an opportunity to lead in a way that makes others follow not because they have to, but because they want to. Because they trust you. Because you move them. Because you embody the vision they long to pursue.

And there—right there—is where true leadership is born.

Building Trust Through Coherence

Trust is the foundation of all solid relationships, and consistency is the tool that builds it day by day. Being consistent means that what we say, do and believe is in alignment, creating a clear and reliable message for those around us. In a world where words often contradict actions, consistency is a beacon of security that inspires respect and strengthens bonds.

How many times have you trusted someone simply because you knew you could count on them to be consistent?

That's the magic of consistency: it builds trust through stability.

Consistency is not about perfection, but about integrity. It means keeping our promises, keeping our word, and acting on our values, even when it's hard. When our actions reflect our intentions, people begin to trust that we are authentic and predictable in our decisions. Ask yourself:

Are my words and actions aligned with the values I want to project?

Perhaps a small adjustment in your consistency could strengthen the key relationships in your life.

Coherence is also built through repetition. Every interaction, no matter how small, reinforces or erodes trust. Being consistent in our responses and behaviors, whether at home, at work or with friends, sends a clear message: *"'You can count on me."* This not only strengthens relationships, but also establishes a solid foundation for overcoming challenges, because people know that you will not change course in the face of adversity.

In leadership, consistency is especially powerful. Teams don't just want inspirational leaders; They want leaders they can trust. Consistent leaders do not say one thing and do another; They lead by example, showing through their actions the values and principles they expect from others. This not only builds respect, but also motivates teams to emulate that behavior.

What kind of message are you sending through your daily actions?

Maybe today is the time to align yourself more with what you want to reflect.

Abraham Lincoln, the 16th President of the United States, is a timeless example of how consistency can be the foundation for building trust, even in the most tumultuous of times. During his presidency, Lincoln led the country through the Civil War, a period of extreme division and suffering. In the midst of chaos, his ability to remain consistent in his principles, actions, and communication not only united a nation, but also cemented his place in history as a leader worthy of trust and respect.

From the beginning of his political career, Lincoln was clear in his stance on equality and justice, even when his views were unpopular. His commitment to the abolition of slavery was a constant that guided his decisions, despite fierce opposition. In every speech and action, Lincoln showed consistency in his purpose: to preserve the Union and ensure liberty for all. This alignment between his values and his decisions inspired confidence, both in his allies and in those who initially doubted him.

Ask yourself:

How aligned are my actions with the values I stand for?

Lincoln's consistency reminds us that leading with integrity leaves a lasting mark.

One of the most emblematic moments of his consistency was the drafting of the Emancipation Proclamation in 1863. Lincoln faced enormous political and social pressures, but remained faithful to his conviction that slavery was morally unacceptable.

This act not only reaffirmed his commitment to equality, but also sent a clear message that he was willing to make difficult decisions to remain consistent with his principles. By acting on what he had promised,

Lincoln strengthened the confidence of his followers and solidified his legacy as a tireless defender of freedom.

Lincoln's coherence was not only reflected in his political decisions, but also in his way of relating to people. He was known for his honesty, a quality that earned him the nickname "Honest Abe." Even in times of disagreement, Lincoln treated his opponents with respect and never compromised his values to win an argument. This approach not only allowed him to build respectful relationships, but also made him an effective mediator capable of unifying opposing factions. His example invites us to reflect:

How could you strengthen trust in your relationships by acting with consistency and respect?

Lincoln also demonstrated that consistency does not mean inflexibility. Although it always remained faithful to its fundamental principles, it adapted its strategies to face the challenges of the moment. This ability to balance firmness in his values with adaptability in his methods showed that consistency is not rigid, but rather a commitment to a greater purpose.

Abraham Lincoln's leadership teaches us that trust is not earned by isolated grand gestures, but by the consistency of our actions over time. His life is a testament to how consistency can overcome divisions, inspire others, and leave a lasting impact.

So, when faced with difficult decisions, ask yourself:

Am I being consistent with my values and my purpose?

Like Lincoln, you may find that leading with consistency not only builds trust, but also paves the way to true, meaningful change.

"The best way to predict the future is to create it."
-Abraham Lincoln-

Building trust through consistency doesn't mean we never make mistakes; It means that when we do, we are honest about it and take steps to correct them. Consistency is not an impossible standard to achieve, but rather an ongoing commitment to acting with integrity and purpose. Every time we show consistency, we strengthen not only our relationships, but also our reputation and our sense of identity.

Ultimately, consistency is the bridge between our intentions and our actions. It allows us to build trust, strengthen relationships and live according to our values. So today, choose to be consistent in your words and actions. Not only for others, but also for yourself, because consistency not only builds confidence; Build a life that reflects who you really are.

What small steps could you take today to be more consistent?

You'll probably find that those consistent, yet simple, actions have the power to transform your relationships and your world.

The Power of Recognition

Recognition has immense power, yet we often underestimate it. Beyond being a courtesy, recognizing someone for their efforts, achievements, or qualities is a transformative act that strengthens relationships, fosters trust and awakens potential in people. It is like a spark that lights the fire of motivation and commitment. When we recognize someone, we are saying: *"I see you. Your work matters. You matter."*

Do you remember the last time someone sincerely appreciated what you did?

That moment probably left a positive mark on your heart.

Recognition is not only a tool to strengthen relationships, but also a means to inspire excellence. When people feel that their efforts are valued, they are more inclined to give their best. This type of motivation is not born from fear or pressure, but from a deep sense of appreciation. On a team, whether at work or in personal life, recognition can be the difference between mediocrity and greatness.

Let me ask you:

¿When was the last time you recognized someone for something they did well?

The power of recognition also lies in its ability to foster a positive culture. In an environment where people feel valued, creativity, collaboration, and trust flourish. It is not necessary to wait for great achievements to recognize someone; small gestures also count. Appreciating daily efforts, unique qualities, or small successes can have a cumulative impact that transforms the dynamic of any group.

¿How would your relationships change if you chose to express more gratitude and recognition today?

Recognizing someone not only benefits the recipient, but also the giver. By focusing on the positive and expressing our appreciation, we strengthen our ability to see value in others and ourselves. This seemingly simple act not only connects, but also reminds us that gratitude is a powerful force for cultivating a fuller, more satisfying life.

Finally, recognition is not just about words; It's also about authenticity. Say *"Good job"* Superficially, it doesn't have the same impact as taking the time to explain why you value what someone did or how it positively impacted you or the group. An authentic recognition has the power to touch the heart of the other person and strengthen the bond that unites them.

Ultimately, the power of recognition lies in its ability to transform relationships, lift spirits, and build stronger communities. So today, take a step forward and recognize someone. It could be a colleague, a friend, a family member, or even a stranger who did something worthy of appreciation. Because when we recognize others, we not only elevate them; We also rise together.

What impact could you have if you made recognition a daily practice?

You may discover that those simple words have the power to change the world, one interaction at a time.

Practical Strategies to Get Others to Follow You

Communicate a Clear Vision: Define and articulate a purpose that inspires others. Make sure it is understandable, relevant and motivating.

　o Example: In a team project, establish specific goals that connect with shared values.

Demonstrate Integrity: Act in accordance with the values you promote. Consistency builds trust and respect.

　o Example: If you preach the importance of punctuality, make sure you are always punctual.

Empower Others: Gives people the tools and autonomy necessary to contribute meaningfully.

　o Example: Delegating important responsibilities demonstrates confidence in the team's abilities.

Practical Exercise: Cultivating Soulful, Inspirational Leadership

Inspirational leadership doesn't begin with a strategy—it begins with an inner vision.
It's not just about directing people; it's about igniting flames: of purpose, of hope, of shared meaning.

This exercise invites you to connect with the essence of your leadership—and turn it into a force that moves not only outcomes… but hearts.

---

1. Define a Vision That Goes Beyond Yourself

Close your eyes for a moment and ask yourself:

- *What do I want to build that benefits not just me, but those around me?*
- *What dream could give direction, energy, and meaning to my leadership?*
- *What does a better future look like because of the impact I can help create?*

Now, write it down in one clear, powerful sentence—one filled with intention.
A sentence you can return to when you feel tired. One that lifts you when others doubt.
Your vision is your guiding light. Let it shine beyond you.

---

2. Identify the Values That Anchor Your Path

Values are not decorations—they are foundations.
List the principles that guide your decisions as a leader:

- Is integrity your compass?
- Or empathy, excellence, justice, authenticity?

Then ask yourself a bold but necessary question:

Am I truly living these values… or merely speaking them?

Where there is alignment, there is inspiration.
Where there is disconnection, trust fades.
Make your values your compass—not just a speech.

---

3. Acknowledge and Appreciate Those Who Walk Beside You

No leader rises alone.
Pause to look around you:

- Who has contributed to your growth—even silently?

- Who has supported your projects without asking for recognition?

- Who deserves your gratitude, even if you've never said it aloud?

Write at least three heartfelt messages of appreciation.
You can send them via text, say them in person, or write them by hand. The format doesn't matter—what matters is that they come from the heart.

Gratitude is the silent energy that nurtures trust, commitment, and belonging.

Final Reflection: Leading with Purpose, Integrity, and Love

As you complete this exercise, reflect on the following:

- What shifted in me when I wrote my vision?

- What did I remember while reviewing my values?

- What did I feel while expressing gratitude to my team?

Remember: to lead with inspiration is not to demand a path—it's to walk it first.
It's to embody a different way of leading: more human, more aligned, more luminous.

Because in the end, **true leadership doesn't just move ideas.**

It moves souls—toward a greater purpose.

Chapter 8:

Emotional Intelligence in Leadership and Relationships

The most powerful connections and the most influential leaders are not those who simply master communication or persuasion strategies, but those who have developed deep emotional intelligence. The ability to recognize, understand and manage our emotions, as well as those of others, allows us to interact with authenticity, empathy, and leadership.

Without emotional intelligence, social, and leadership skills can become mechanical, empty, and ineffective. The key to building strong relationships and leading with impact lies not only in what we do, but in how we emotionally relate to others.

Understanding Emotional Intelligence: The Key to Leadership and Authentic Relationships

Emotional intelligence is much more than just a social skill; It is the foundation upon which our relationships, our leadership abilities, and our own personal growth are built. In a world where information is abundant, but authentic connection is scarce, developing emotional intelligence allows us to not only understand ourselves better, but also connect with others in deeper and more meaningful ways.

The term *emotional intelligence* It was popularized by the psychologist *Daniel Goleman*, who demonstrated that success in life and leadership does not depend solely on intelligence quotient (IQ), but on our ability to manage our emotions and understand those of others. People with high emotional intelligence not only navigate life's challenges better, they also build stronger relationships, inspire trust, and lead with empathy.

But what does it really mean to have emotional intelligence?

To understand it thoroughly, we need to explore its five fundamental pillars: **self-awareness, self-regulation, motivation, empathy** and **social skills**. Each of these elements acts as a key piece in the way we experience the world and relate to it.

Self-awareness: Know Yourself

Self-awareness is the cornerstone of emotional intelligence. It means being aware of our emotions, recognizing how they influence our thoughts and behaviors, and understanding our strengths and areas for improvement. A person with high self-awareness does not allow themselves to be carried away by their emotions without understanding them; instead, it observes them and analyzes their impact.

Think about a time when you reacted impulsively to a situation and later regretted it. That lack of self-awareness prevented you from recognizing how your emotions were influencing your response.

Now imagine that you have the ability to stop, evaluate the situation, and choose the best way to respond. That is the power of **self-awareness**- Gives you control over your life instead of allowing emotions to take control of you.

For a week, keep an emotional diary. Every time you experience a strong emotion (whether positive or negative), write it down and reflect on what caused it and how it influenced your actions. This simple habit can help you develop greater awareness of your emotional patterns.

Self-regulation: Manage Your Emotions with Intelligence

Self-regulation is the ability to control our emotions instead of allowing them to control us. It does not mean repressing what we feel, but learning to channel our emotions in a constructive way.

People with high self-regulation do not react impulsively; Instead, they take a breath, analyze the situation, and choose the best response. This skill is especially crucial in leadership and interpersonal relationships.

A leader who loses his cool easily and reacts with anger or frustration creates a tense environment, while a leader who manages his emotions intelligently generates trust and respect.

Imagine you are in a meeting and someone criticizes an idea you presented. The impulsive reaction would be to immediately defend yourself, feeling attacked.

But a person high in self-regulation would take a moment to process the criticism, asking themselves if there is anything valuable in it, and responding calmly. This skill not only avoids unnecessary conflict, but also opens the door to learning and continuous improvement.

I invite you to practice the technique of **five seconds**. Whenever you are faced with a situation that triggers an intense emotion, take a deep breath and count to five before responding. This small habit will give you the time necessary to choose a more conscious and effective reaction.

Motivation: The Engine that Will Drive You to Continue Growing

Motivation is the fuel that drives us to act, to improve and to achieve our goals. Without motivation, even highly talented people can stay stuck, while those who are talented find a way to overcome any obstacle.

The key to strong motivation is having a clear purpose. People with high emotional intelligence are not motivated solely by external rewards (money, recognition, status), but by an internal motivation that gives meaning to what they do.

As a recommendation, write a list of three things that motivate you deeply in life. Then, reflect on how you can align your daily actions with those motivations.

Empathy: Connecting with Others on a Deeper Level

As we have mentioned previously, empathy is the ability to understand and feel what others are experiencing. It's not just about understanding their words, but about capturing their emotions and perspectives. Empathy allows us to connect authentically, strengthen our relationships, and resolve conflicts more easily.

People with high empathy don't just listen; They really pay attention. They pick up on body language, tones of voice, and emotional cues that others may miss. This allows them to respond more effectively and build relationships based on trust.

In a difficult conversation, instead of responding with judgment or defense, an empathetic person asks questions like: *"I understand this is important to you, can you tell me more about how you feel?"* This simple question can transform an argument into an opportunity to deepen the relationship.

In your next conversation, make a conscious effort to actively listen without interrupting. Then, repeat in your own words what the other person said to make sure you understood them correctly.

Social Skills: Build Relationships with Emotional Intelligence

Social skills are the culmination of all the previous pillars. A person with high emotional intelligence knows how to communicate effectively, resolve conflicts, inspire others, and work as a team.

In leadership, social skills are essential. A leader who knows how to motivate his team, build trust, and tactfully resolve differences will have much more impact than someone who only focuses on results without considering human relationships.

As an example, let's remember that Satya Nadella transformed Microsoft's culture by prioritizing collaboration and innovation through empathy and effective communication. Its approach based on emotional intelligence allowed the company to reinvent itself and become a market leader again.

In your next professional interaction, make a conscious effort to show genuine appreciation and recognition toward someone. See how this small gesture strengthens the relationship and generates a positive response.

Developing emotional intelligence is not an overnight process, but every small effort you make to improve your self-awareness, self-regulation, motivation, empathy, and social skills has a profound impact on your life and the people around you.

It is important that at every opportunity you are always asking yourself:

How can I apply these pillars in my daily life?

The answer to that question can make the difference between superficial relationships and deep connections, between ordinary leadership and truly transformative leadership.

Because at the end of the day, true success is not measured only in achievements, but in the quality of our relationships and the impact we leave on others. And emotional intelligence is the tool that allows you to build that legacy.

Self-awareness and Self-regulation: The Foundation of Personal Leadership

Personal leadership begins with the ability to know yourself and manage your emotions effectively. Self-awareness and self-regulation not only impact how we relate to others, but also determine the quality of our decisions, our resilience in the face of challenges, and our ability to lead with integrity. A leader who does not know himself is like a ship without a rudder, at the mercy of circumstances. But a leader who cultivates self-awareness and practices self-regulation has the power to navigate any storm with clarity and purpose.

The **self-awareness** It is the ability to recognize and understand our emotions, our thinking patterns, and the way they affect our actions. It involves identifying our strengths, our weaknesses and our deep motivations. A leader with high self-awareness does not allow himself to be carried away by unconscious impulses, but rather observes his own reactions and consciously adjusts them.

Ask yourself:

> **How do I react under pressure? What emotions guide my decisions? How do others perceive my leadership?**

The answer to these questions is key to knowing yourself better and enhancing your ability to positively influence others.

However, self-awareness without **self-regulation** It's like having a map without knowing how to use it. Self-regulation is the ability to manage our emotions instead of having them control us. It does not mean repressing what we feel, but learning to channel those emotions productively. An emotionally reactive leader can generate distrust, while a leader who knows how to manage his frustration, impatience, or stress inspires stability and confidence in his team.

Imagine yourself in a situation where things don't go as you expected. A leader without self-regulation could react with anger, guilt or demotivation, affecting the environment and morale of his team. Instead, a leader with high self-regulation will take a moment to process their emotions before responding, seeking solutions instead of generating conflict.

Ask yourself the following question:

How can I better manage my emotions during difficult times?

This level of control not only improves your leadership, but also strengthens your relationships and your ability to effectively solve problems.

Developing self-awareness and self-regulation is a process that requires constant practice. You can start with small actions, such as taking a few seconds to breathe before responding in a difficult conversation, reflecting on your emotional reactions, or keeping a journal where you record how you felt in key situations. The key is not to judge yourself, but to learn from each experience and make adjustments that help you lead with greater awareness.

When a leader masters self-awareness and self-regulation, his or her leadership becomes more authentic, trustworthy, and balanced. You no longer react impulsively, but act with intention. He or she does not give in to stress or pressure, but rather stands firm in his values and vision. And most importantly, it creates an environment where others can also learn to manage their emotions and lead from a place of balance and clarity. Because in the end, personal leadership is not about controlling others, but about learning to lead ourselves first.

Empathy as a Pillar of Emotional Intelligence

Empathy is the invisible bridge that unites people, the silent language that says *"I see you, I hear you, I understand you"*. At the heart of emotional intelligence, empathy is the skill that allows us to connect with others on a deep level, understand their emotions, and respond sensitively. It is not just about sympathizing with the other, but about putting yourself in their place, feeling what they feel and acting with understanding. In a world where communication has become instantaneous, but often superficial, developing empathy is more important than ever.

Empathy is not simply a personality trait; It is a skill that is cultivated with intention. It means listening beyond words, perceiving body language, gestures, and silences that reveal what is regularly not said. An empathetic leader not only cares about results, but also about the well-being of his team. An empathetic friend not only hears problems, but understands them from the other person's perspective.

Let's think about it for a moment:

How many times in your daily interactions do you really take the time to listen with your heart and not just your ears?

One of the biggest challenges with empathy is learning to see it as a strength and not a vulnerability. In a competitive environment, many people believe that showing empathy is letting our guard down, when in reality it is one of the most powerful tools for influence and human connection.

People feel more motivated and committed to those who value and understand them. The most memorable leaders are not those who dictate orders, but those who create a space where each person feels that their voice matters.

Developing empathy requires leaving our own perspective and seeing the world from the eyes of the other. This means practicing active listening, asking open-ended questions, showing genuine interest, and avoiding hasty judgments. It also means recognizing that each person has their own story, their own fears and internal struggles that can influence their behavior. Empathy helps us replace criticism with understanding, indifference with support, and distance with true connection.

Empathy not only improves our relationships, it also makes us better leaders, better friends, and better human beings. It allows us to build strong teams, resolve conflicts more easily and be a source of inspiration for others. So today, make the conscious effort to look beyond the obvious, to listen with intention and to connect from understanding. Because when you choose to be empathetic, you not only impact the lives of others, but you also transform your own.

How could you practice empathy more in your daily life?

Perhaps the key to improving your relationships and leadership is not in talking more, but in listening better.

Emotional Intelligence as an Essential Skill

Emotional intelligence is not only a useful tool to improve our relationships or perform better in leadership; It is an essential skill for navigating life with success and purpose. In a world where human interactions are marked by speed, pressure and uncertainty, being emotionally intelligent allows us to stand firm in the midst of chaos, connect with authenticity and respond to challenges with clarity and balance.

Every day we face situations that test our emotional intelligence: a difficult conversation, a disagreement at work, a moment of frustration with a loved one. How we choose to respond to these situations determines the quality of our relationships and the impact we leave on others.

Ask yourself:

Am I reacting impulsively, or choosing my responses with awareness and purpose?

The difference between both options defines the kind of leader and human being you are.

Emotional intelligence is not a gift we are born with or not; It is a skill that is developed with practice, reflection and commitment. It means learning to recognize our emotions without being dominated, to see others' perspective before judging, and to build relationships based on trust and understanding. It is not about avoiding conflicts or difficult emotions, but about managing them wisely, transforming them into opportunities for growth.

If you want to positively influence others, you must start with yourself. Mastering emotional intelligence is not a destination, but a constant process of self-knowledge and improvement. It requires the courage to look inward, to accept our areas of improvement, and to commit to leading with empathy, integrity, and balance.

Therefore, ask yourself the following questions:

How can I be more aware of my emotions?

How can I listen better?

How can I inspire more authentically?

The true power of emotional intelligence lies in its ability to transform our lives from the inside out. It allows us to build deeper connections, resolve conflicts maturely, and become leaders who inspire not by what they say, but by how they live. So today, make the decision to develop this skill with intention. Because when you choose to lead with emotional intelligence, you not only change your life, but you also have the power to transform the world around you.

Chapter 9:

Leadership as a Commitment to Others

True leadership is not a pedestal to stand out, but a bridge that connects, elevates and transforms. Leading is not about exercising power over others, but about being of service to them. It is an ongoing commitment to leading with purpose, empathy, and a clear vision of the impact you can have on the lives of those around you. Leading with a commitment to others is a daily choice that reflects not only who you are, but also what you believe in and how you decide to make a difference.

Lead from Service

Effective leadership begins with service. When you lead from a place of humility and generosity, you not only inspire trust, but you also build relationships that transcend the transactional. Leading from service means recognizing that collective success is more important than individual success, and that your role as a leader is to create an environment where everyone can thrive.

Leading from service is not just a strategy; It is a call to act from the heart. It is looking beyond titles and hierarchies to recognize the humanity in others, to see in each person their potential and in each interaction an opportunity to create something greater than ourselves. Serving as a leader does not mean giving up authority, but rather using it to empower, inspire and guide.

Do an introspection:

What impact are you having on those around you?

Probably, That impact can be multiplied if you choose to lead from a place of service.

A servant leader is one who listens before speaking, who understands before acting, and who prioritizes the well-being of his team above his own comfort. This type of leadership creates an environment where people feel valued and respected, which in turn awakens the best in them.

Leading from service does not mean carrying all the weight, but rather sharing it, creating a space where everyone can contribute and shine. By choosing to serve, you not only create better relationships, but also a shared purpose that unites and therefore motivates.

When you decide to lead from service, you send a powerful message: ***"I'm here for you. I'm with you."*** This act of humility and generosity builds trust and breaks down barriers. People don't follow a leader just because of what he says, but because of how he makes them feel. And nothing inspires more than knowing that someone is committed to your success and well-being.

In a world where results are often prioritized over people, leading from service is a reminder that true success is measured in the lives we transform.

Leading from service also transforms ourselves. It forces us to look beyond our own needs and ask ourselves:

How can I help others reach their full potential?

This approach not only improves relationships, but also connects us with our best version, the one that acts with empathy, integrity, and purpose. Because in the end, by serving others, we are not only helping; we are growing, learning and leaving a legacy of love and compassion.

Today, you have the opportunity to lead from service. It doesn't matter if you are in charge of a team, a family or simply your own decisions. Every gesture counts. Every word can make a difference.

So pause and reflect:

What can I do today to lead with more service and empathy?

I'm sure you'll find out that by prioritizing others, you find a greater purpose, a deeper connection, and a more fulfilling life. Because leading from service not only changes others; it also changes you.

Building Trust Through Coherence

Trust is any leader's most valuable currency, and it is built through consistency. When your actions reflect your words and values, people feel like they can trust you. No matter how great the adversity, a leader who acts consistently becomes an anchor in times of uncertainty.

Trust is the foundation of all meaningful relationships, whether in personal or professional life. But how is that trust built? The answer is not in big speeches or empty promises, but in coherence, in that constant act of aligning our words, our actions, and our values. Consistency is not just something that is demonstrated in important moments; It is what we show day after day.

I want you to take a moment to think about it:

Do your actions reflect the words you share with those who trust you?

If there are doubts, it is never too late to align what you say with what you do.

Being consistent does not mean being perfect. We are all human, and mistakes are inevitable. But coherence lies in how we respond to those mistakes, in how we face our failures with humility and a willingness to correct them.

When we admit our mistakes instead of justifying them, we send a clear message: *"You can trust me because I am authentic, and I am willing to improve."* This simple but powerful act not only strengthens trust, but also demonstrates our integrity.

Every interaction, no matter how small, is an opportunity to build or erode trust. Coherence does not always manifest itself in grand gestures, but in the constancy of our small actions. It's showing up on time when we say we will, keeping a seemingly trivial promise, or simply listening carefully when someone needs us. These repeated actions are what form the solid foundation of trusting relationships.

Let's analyze it for a moment:

How can you demonstrate consistency today in your most important relationships?

Consistency also creates security. When we are consistent in our behavior, the people around us know what to expect from us. This not only builds trust, but also fosters an environment of respect and collaboration. In contrast, inconsistency creates doubt, confusion, and ultimately distance.

Being consistent is a way of saying: *"I'm here for you, and you can count on me."*

How much deeper would your relationships be if your every word was backed by your actions?

Building trust through consistency not only benefits those around you; It also enriches your life. It allows you to live in alignment with your values, reducing internal tensions and increasing your sense of purpose. So today, take a step forward and choose to be consistent.

Take a moment to reflect and ask yourself:

What can I do today to make my actions speak louder than my words?

By doing so, you will not only strengthen your relationships, but you will also connect with a more authentic and powerful version of yourself. Because in the end, consistency doesn't just build trust; build a legacy of integrity and respect that transcends time.

Inspiring with Purpose

A committed leader not only guides; inspire. Your purpose as a leader should not be limited to directing actions, but to ignite passions. People want to feel part of something bigger, and you have the power to show them that vision.

Leading with purpose is not about giving orders, but rather painting a clear picture of what is possible and encouraging others to join that mission.

Inspiring with purpose is much more than motivating others; It is igniting a spark that illuminates their path and connects them with something bigger than themselves. It is an act of service that transcends words and reaches the heart.

When you lead with purpose, your actions not only have personal meaning, but resonate with those around you, creating a lasting impact.

Ask yourself the following:

What purpose is guiding your words and actions?

You will most likely find in that answer the key to inspiring in a deeper and more authentic way.

Inspiring is not a selfish act; It's a gift. It requires clarity about what truly matters, because inspiration without purpose dissipates quickly. When your actions reflect a clear and meaningful vision, those around you not only follow you, but also adopt that purpose as their own. This type of leadership transforms groups into communities and individual efforts into collective movements.

Reflect with me:

How can you align your goals with a greater purpose?

That alignment is what turns an ordinary leader into an extraordinary one.

Purpose doesn't need to be great to be powerful. Sometimes inspiring with purpose simply means helping someone see their own value or showing them that their effort matters. It's a reminder that even small gestures have a profound impact. A word of encouragement, an act of kindness, or an example of resilience can transform someone's perspective in their darkest moments.

Go deeper:

What small act of inspiration could you do today to make a difference?

You also need to be vulnerable. Sharing your own challenges, failures, and learnings does not diminish your leadership; humanizes it. People don't connect with unattainable ideals, but with real stories. By showing them not only your successes, but also your struggles, you teach them that purpose does not come from perfection, but from perseverance.

Ask yourself:

What aspects of your story can inspire others to overcome their own obstacles?

By sharing them, you can turn your scars into maps for those seeking their own path.

Ultimately, inspiring with purpose is not about you, but the impact you leave on others. It is a commitment to lead with integrity, to act with intentionality, and to remember that every interaction is an opportunity to positively influence.

Today, reflect:

How can you lead from your purpose and ignite that of others?

You may find that by inspiring in this way, you not only transform the lives of those around you, but you also find deeper meaning in your own. Because leading with purpose is, at its core, a way of living with purpose.

Your Commitment as a Leader

Leading with impact requires dedication, authenticity, and a constant willingness to grow. It's not about how many people follow you, but how many lives you can transform. As a leader, you have the power to leave a legacy that inspires others to lead as well.

Leading is not a destiny; It is a continuous journey. It's a choice you make every day, a commitment to something bigger than yourself. Being a leader does not mean having all the answers, but rather being the person willing to take the first step towards significant change. It is being there, even when it is difficult, even when the path is unclear, because you know that your impact can transform not only those around you, but also the world.

Ask yourself:

What mark do I want to leave as a leader?

Because in that answer lies your true purpose.

Leading with impact begins with a promise: to be consistent with your values, authentic in your actions, and generous in your service. People don't follow titles, they follow hearts, and when you lead from the heart, you create a space where others can flourish. Think about the people who have trusted you, who have sought your guidance or support. They see you as a beacon, someone who can illuminate their path.

How can you be that leader who inspires, motivates and transforms?

The commitment to lead is not easy, but it is deeply rewarding. It means being willing to take responsibility, face challenges, and stand firm on your values, even when the world seems to pull you in another direction. But it also means celebrating the achievements of others, witnessing their growth, and knowing that your influence, though sometimes invisible, is leaving a lasting impact.

Visualize yourself and ask the following question:

How do I want to be remembered by those I lead?

That memory will be your legacy.

Beyond goals and results, leading is an act of connection. It is touching people's lives in a way that uplifts them, inspires them, and gives them hope. It's showing them that, even in the darkest moments, there is a light we can turn on together.

Leading is a commitment to shared humanity, with the idea that, by coming together, we can overcome any obstacle.

Ask yourself:

What else can I do today to connect with those around me and guide them towards their best version?

Today, and every day, you have the opportunity to choose how to lead. You can lead with love, with purpose, with the intention of building something that transcends time and circumstances. So look within, look for that spark that moves you, and commit to being the leader the world needs. Not because you have to, but because you know that is your calling.

Because by leading with your whole being, you not only change lives; you find the true meaning of leadership.

Are you ready to accept this commitment and start leading with your heart?

The time is now, and the impact you can create... is infinite.

Final Chapter:

Connecting to Lead with Impact

Throughout this book, we have explored the fundamental principles that build meaningful relationships, inspire others, and make us authentic leaders. From the art of winning friends to the ability to positively influence and mobilize those around us, it is clear that leadership is not a destination, but a constant journey of learning and growth.

Reflecting on the Power of Connection

In an increasingly interconnected world, the ability to build and maintain genuine relationships has become an essential skill. We have learned that empathy, authenticity, and vulnerability are not only human virtues, but also powerful tools for leadership. Stories like those of Florence Nightingale, Theodore Roosevelt, and Mary McLeod Bethune remind us that by leading with the heart, we can overcome barriers and create lasting change.

The power of connection is the thread that binds our lives together, a constant reminder that we are not alone in this vast world. Every interaction, no matter how small, is an opportunity to forge bonds that strengthen us, inspire us and transform us.

Connecting with others is not just a basic human need; It is a force that enriches our experiences and drives us to reach our full potential. How many times has a meaningful connection changed your day, your outlook, or even your life?

The connection goes beyond words; It is an act of presence, an exchange of emotions and a recognition of our shared humanity. In a world where distractions are constant, choosing to connect with intention is an act of love and courage. It is looking into the eyes, listening carefully and responding with the heart.

Don't forget to always ask yourself:

How many authentic connections have I cultivated lately?

At best, and The first step is to slow down at that moment and be truly present.

The power of connection also reminds us that our differences are not barriers, but rather bridges to a deeper, more unique understanding. By opening ourselves to the stories, struggles, and triumphs of others, we broaden our perspective and strengthen our empathy.

Every authentic connection challenges us to be more compassionate, to find common ground, and to celebrate what unites us rather than what separates us.

What would happen if today you chose to see differences as opportunities to learn and grow?

Connecting not only benefits our relationships, but also our own health and well-being. Studies have shown that meaningful connections reduce stress, improve mental health, and make us more resilient in the face of challenges. But beyond the individual benefits, connection reminds us that we are part of something bigger: a web of intertwined lives that together have the power to change the world.

Reflecting on the power of connection is also an invitation to value what we already have. We often take the people around us for granted, forgetting the impact they have on our lives.

What would change if today you chose to express gratitude for those connections?

Maybe a simple *"Thank you for being here"* It could deepen a relationship or even heal a distance.

Ultimately, the power of connection reminds us that we are not designed to walk alone. Every interaction, every relationship, is an opportunity to give and receive, to build and strengthen.

So today, reflect:

How are you using the power of connection in your life?

Because surely, by connecting with others, you also find a deeper connection with yourself. Because in the act of connecting, we not only find company; we find meaning, purpose, and a greater understanding of what it means to be human together.

Now it's your turn to ask yourself:

How am I applying these principles in my daily life?

Am I building bridges or raising barriers?

Do my communication and actions reflect the values I wish to promote?

Leadership as a Commitment to Others

True leadership is not measured by titles or positions, but by the impact we generate in the lives of others. It is a deep commitment to guide, inspire and serve, placing the needs of those we lead above our own.

Leading is not a privilege to be enjoyed; It is a responsibility that is assumed with humility and purpose.

Dare to ask yourself:

How am I using my influence to improve the lives of those around me?

It could be that The leadership you seek begins with this commitment.

Being a leader does not mean having all the answers, but rather being willing to listen, learn and act for the benefit of others. It is recognizing that leadership is not about controlling, but about empowering.

A committed leader is one who sees the potential in every person and works tirelessly to help them achieve it. When you choose to lead with this approach, you not only inspire trust, but you also build relationships based on respect and collaboration.

Commitment to others also involves making difficult decisions when necessary, but always with integrity and empathy. A true leader is not afraid to face challenges or say what is right, even when it is unpopular. This type of leadership, guided by strong values and a clear vision, not only leads, but also unifies.

What decisions are you making today that reflect your commitment to the well-being of others?

Furthermore, leadership as a commitment to others means being present, even in the most difficult moments. It's not just about leading in times of success, but about standing by your team when they face challenges.

It is in those moments where a leader's character truly shines, showing that no matter how difficult the road is, they will be there to support, guide and move forward together.

And leading as a commitment to others is an act of generosity. It's recognizing that the most lasting impact you can have is not in what you accomplish individually, but in how you inspire and uplift others. When you lead from a place of service, you leave a legacy that goes beyond your time and your presence.

Ultimately, leadership as a commitment to others is not an easy path, but it is deeply rewarding. It's an opportunity to leave the world better than you found it, to be the force that drives others towards their dreams, and to build stronger, more connected communities.

So today, take a moment to breathe and reflect:

How can you lead with greater commitment to others?

By assuming that responsibility, you will surely discover that the true power of leadership is not in what you receive, but in what you give.

Your Next Steps as a Connected Leader

The knowledge you have acquired in this book is worthless if you do not put it into practice. So I encourage you to take a moment to consider how you can apply these lessons starting today:

Evaluate your Current Relationships: Identify which ones need strengthening and which ones could become strategic alliances. Make a plan to improve and deepen those connections.

Define your Vision: Clearly articulate what you want to achieve and how your values guide that purpose. Write it down and share it with the people around you.

Act with Empathy and Authenticity: Make a conscious effort to actively listen, communicate transparently, and lead by example.

Final Exercise: Your Manifesto of Connection and Leadership

Authentic leadership isn't measured by the titles you hold—but by the footprints you leave behind.

This final exercise is an invitation to crystallize your path as a conscious leader—to turn everything you've learned into a living manifesto that inspires you each day and reminds you why you chose to lead from the soul.

---

1. Write Your Purpose as a Conscious Leader

Pause. Breathe. Close your eyes.
Visualize the impact you wish to leave, long after your presence becomes an echo in the hearts of others.

Now, write one paragraph that answers honestly:

- What drives your leadership?

- What kind of transformation do you wish to create in others, in your community, in the world?

- How do you want to be remembered by those who walked beside you?

Write it from the heart—no filters, no need for perfection.
This purpose will become your inner compass when doubt clouds the way.

---

2. Identify Your Guiding Principles

Every leader requires deep roots.
Choose **three core values** that will guide how you act, decide, and serve.
For example:

- *Compassion, Truth, Courage*

- *Integrity, Service, Humility*

- *Authenticity, Presence, Purpose*

Don't choose them to sound impressive. Choose them because they are

you.
These principles are your anchor when ego or fear try to pull you off course.

---

3. Make a Concrete Commitment to Action

Leadership doesn't live in lofty visions—it lives in daily choices.
Decide on **one specific action** you will take this week to strengthen a relationship or inspire someone around you.
It can be something small, yet meaningful:

- Having an honest conversation you've been postponing.

- Listening with full presence to someone who needs it.

- Expressing deep gratitude to someone who has shaped your path.

Give it a date, a method, and a clear intention.
Because change doesn't happen through intention alone—it happens through movement.

Final Reflection: Your Manifesto Is Alive

This is not an ending.
It is the beginning of a new chapter—one where you choose to lead with love, alignment, and connection.

Remember:
Leadership does not demand perfection. Only commitment.
Every step you take toward authentic connection is a win.
Every moment you live your values—you light the way for others.

> **You don't just lead with your words.**
> **You lead with your example.**
> **You lead with your presence.**

You lead with your humanity.

A Commitment to Lead with Impact

Leading with impact is not just an aspiration; It is a deep commitment to leaving a meaningful mark on the lives of others. It is the conscious decision to turn every action, every word and every decision into a catalyst for positive change. Nor does it mean seeking perfection, but rather acting with purpose and authenticity, inspiring others to be their best selves.

Ask yourself:

What impact am I leaving on the people and world around me?

Perhaps that is the starting point for leading with renewed purpose.

A leader's impact is not only measured by tangible results, but also by how he or she makes people feel. A leader with impact knows that his influence goes beyond the goals achieved and resides in the connection he builds with those who follow him. This type of leadership is not about imposing, but about empowering; not to control, but to inspire.

How can you use your leadership today to uplift those around you?

Leading with impact requires clarity of purpose. A committed leader understands why he is leading and where he wants to lead his team or community. This purpose acts as a compass, guiding your decisions and giving meaning to your actions. When others see that clarity and conviction, they are drawn to the leader's vision, which strengthens collaboration and commitment.

Think about it for a moment and ask yourself the following question:

What purpose drives my leadership?

By answering this question, you will be taking a step towards a more significant impact.

The commitment to leading with impact also involves courage to make decisions that transcend self-interest and benefit others. This may mean standing up for what is right in times of controversy, prioritizing your team's well-being over your comfort, or taking risks to drive meaningful change.

A leader with impact is not afraid of challenge; sees it as an opportunity to grow and make a difference.

Finally, leading with impact means constantly reflecting on the legacy you are building.

How do you want to be remembered?

Every interaction, every decision, and every challenge you face contributes to that legacy. Leading with impact is not about being perfect, but about acting with integrity, empathy, and an unwavering commitment to the common good.

It is an opportunity to inspire, transform and contribute to something bigger than ourselves. So today, choose to lead with intention.

Pause and reflect:

What can I do today to make a positive impact on the lives I touch?

By leading with impact, you not only change others, but you also transform your own life in the process.

Connecting and leading is not a linear or simple process, but it is deeply rewarding. Every conversation, every relationship, and every action is an opportunity to make a difference.

As John C. Maxwell once said:

"A leader is one who knows the path, walks it, and shows the path to

others."

This book is an invitation to walk that path, learning and evolving as you lead with purpose. Thank you for accompanying me on this beautiful journey towards more human and meaningful leadership.

Now, you write the next chapter.

ABOUT THE AUTHOR

Ezra Muri (Ezra Martínez Murillo) is a passionate leader, committed to personal growth and the well-being of others. His life is marked by an optimistic vision, a deep ambition to improve himself, and an unwavering desire to help those around him. As author of *The Power of Connecting*, Ezra shares his transformative journey and provides practical tools, so people can develop authentic connections, overcome social barriers, and unleash their full potential.

From an early age, Ezra demonstrated an innate talent for communication, winning state championships in speech and political debate at the age of fourteen. However, his own path to trust and connection was not easy. Despite his ability to speak and act fluently, he struggled with insecurities and social challenges that distanced him from his surroundings. It was this personal experience that prompted him to seek a profound change in his life.

At age twenty, Ezra began a path of self-discovery as a holistic therapist, dedicating himself to guiding group meditations, spiritual journeys, and conferences on spiritual and energy healing. His approach based on empathy and love led him to help countless people overcome internal blocks and reconnect with themselves. This period not only enriched his life, but also cemented his passion for empowering others.

His journey continued in Vancouver, Canada, where multicultural dynamics led him to hone his communication and leadership skills. These experiences, coupled with his desire to help close friends with extraordinary potential but limited by a lack of social skills, inspired him to write *The Power of Connecting*. This book is a testament to his love and commitment to those who want to build meaningful relationships and become inspirational leaders.

Ezra sees himself not only as an author, but as a friend and mentor who is present to guide his readers in their transformation. Through his work, he offers practical strategies for communicating, resolving conflict, and connecting authentically, all with a focus on empathy and respect. With an accessible style and a deep desire to serve, Ezra seeks to open doors where there were once walls, both personally and professionally.

With *The Power of Connecting*, Ezra reaffirms its mission to positively influence people's lives, helping them find their voice, strengthen their relationships and reach their full potential. His message is clear: we all have the ability to lead, inspire and transform, and he is here to guide us on that path.

www.ingramcontent.com/pod-product-compliance
Lightning Source LLC
Chambersburg PA
CBHW050435010526
44118CB00013B/1536